BRIGHTON'S
OUTSKIRTS
PEOPLE, PLACE, COMMUNITY

ARCHIVES ALIVE

QueenSpark Books was formed in 1972 and has published over 110 books on Brighton and Hove that chronicle the city's social history across the past 100 years, in people's own words. We have a unique archive of fascinating and important information, and Archives Alive – a project funded by The National Lottery Heritage Fund – makes these stories accessible again.

Brighton's Outskirts – people, place, community is one of four Archives Alive books published by QueenSpark Books in July 2019. It has been edited and produced by volunteers. With guidance from industry professionals, the volunteer editors chose a theme to explore, and selected content from QueenSpark's online archive and elsewhere.

Other volunteers researched photographic sites for images to accompany the text. Editors selected photographs and worked with designers on layout and design of the books.

Archives Alive also enabled volunteers to identify old documents, slides and letters. This material improves access to heritage material via our website and is permanently deposited at The Keep for public accessibility. www.thekeep.info

In 2019-2020, we are engaging communities across the city, using Archives Alive books to stimulate reading and as a starting point for conversations about our shared heritage. We hope those discussions lead to more stories being told – and that QueenSpark Books publishes people's reflections for many years to come.

We are very grateful to all of our volunteers, who have worked incredibly hard to make this historical material new, and relevant again.

Please enjoy.

QueenSpark Books

Foreword

Brighton's Outskirts – people, place, community began at the first meeting for people interested in working on the Archives Alive project. Sitting together on sofas by the bar, a group of us spoke about the boundaries of our city – its borders and edges; the places between brick walls and the woods.

Michèle and I talked about bus travel and lost railway stations, old communities, new estates and marginalised lives. From this meeting of interests, the theme of outskirts was formed.

With guidance from the Archives Alive project coordinator, Ali Ghanimi, Michèle and I explored QueenSpark Books' archives. We looked for the extracts we felt brought us closer to the authors – to the places and events they remembered.

We read about lives lived away from our city centre's bright lights. We talked about the pull our city exerted on people searching for something better. Sometimes these memories were poignant; sometimes they made us laugh. We enjoyed sharing between us the details that lived on in the pages of old books.

This process of discovery continued with Michèle and I visiting places described in stories we read. The act of taking photographs on our journeys felt like a gathering of evidence, allowing us to capture contemporary echoes of past events, locations and people.

Brighton's Outskirts includes a path lined by railway sleepers and the view from a garden in Bevendean. The corner shop that used to sell lemonade and raspberry powder by the ha'p'orth is here too. These places are landmarks.

We can follow the route of a girl's long walk home from school to a newly built estate far beyond the end of the bus routes. We can stand in a cemetery and remember reading about a boy who played there with his friends.

Outskirts sees Brighton as a changing, physical space and a place occupied by memory. We hope this book will make the archives come alive for you.

Vicky Waters

----

06 - Introduction

07 - Shoreham

09 - Portslade

16 - Devil's Dyke and The Downs

22 - Hove

36 - Withdean and Patcham

40 - Preston Park

46 - Hollingbury

50 - Coldean

53 - Moulsecoomb

64 - Hollingdean

68 - Elm Grove and Bear Road

74 - Bevendean & Racehill

83 - Whitehawk

89 - Black Rock

92 - Woodingdean

96 - Rottingdean

104 - Saltdean

108 - Peacehaven

Introduction

Vicky and I were interested in gathering stories from the QueenSpark Book archives of places, communities, people living on the edges of Brighton and the margins of society. These snippets for *Outskirts* gave us tantalising glimpses into past lives that exist only in memories.

The physical clues that remain come to life through people's stories and connect us with their world. A tangled lump of concrete at Devil's Dyke is a memorial to the Edwardian funfairs, funicular railway and elevated cableway. A platform kerbstone buried in the undergrowth from a long gone railway station – a reminder of where hundreds of people, dressed in their Sunday best, packed like sardines in a steam train, alighted to enjoy a day in the country. People from nearby estates spending many happy hours at a magnificent outdoor swimming pool, which rose from the site of a former rubbish tip and has again returned to wasteland between land and sea.

QueenSpark Books gives voice to people from diverse backgrounds and communities, and we found that many stories were linked over time through place – and displacement. Tight-knit communities from the centre of Brighton were dispersed in the slum clearances of the 1930s and 1950s when people were moved to newly built 'garden estates' on the outskirts of Brighton.

People attracted by Brighton's reputation of tolerance and liberal attitudes included those who had been displaced from elsewhere because of persecution and war as well as transient populations of students and seasonal workers. Many visitors were drawn to Brighton – people down for a 'gay' weekend, a dip in the sea, a day at the races. Local people also enjoyed the distraction of the races – or a picnic in the cemetery, or digging the allotment, or a weekend away in Coldean!

The constant flux of people moving to and from the city rubbing along with those born and bred here is what makes Brighton such a special place. We want to take you on a journey round the outskirts of Brighton through these fascinating stories of everyday experiences, of people making the best of life, however hard.

In *Outskirts*, we include a map of our journey travelled. We hope the map, the images and extracts we have selected will inspire you to explore Brighton as well as to read the publications from QueenSpark Books.

Michèle Allardyce

SHOREHAM

MAP GRID REF: 3A

COLLECTING BREAD IN A PILLOWCASE FROM THE ARMY CAMP

"There was a large army camp at Shoreham during the First World War. There were huts, tents, field kitchens and troops by the thousands. Some of the children in Ellen Street used to be sent by their parents with a pillowcase to walk to Shoreham Camp and back again before school to collect bread, which the soldiers used to slip over the fence to them. I must admit this was something our family did not have to do, although bread was scarce. Later I stood at the end of Ellen Street at the junction of Sackville Road to watch these soldiers marching in fours on their way to Newhaven Harbour. It took hours for them to pass by; they kept in step by whistling some tune. I wonder how many of these men came back."

Ernie Mason
A Working Man – A Century of Hove Memories

OLD SHOREHAM ROAD CARRIAGE WORKS, 1920S

"The trams weren't thought to be a specially good part of the job. They were an arrangement with Brighton Corporation to make trade really. The railwaymen kept the town going. They were the biggest asset in the town. There was a terrible to do when they moved our carriage side to Lancing, in about 1921 or 1922. They moved the whole of the Old Shoreham Road carriage works to Lancing and that meant that there were eight or nine hundred men fewer in Brighton, working in Lancing. It made Lancing into a town. Houses were being sold there for £500 and they came round and pleaded with men to go. If a railwayman was going to buy a house he only had to make a deposit of £25. Those houses are probably worth £12,000 now. The only people who made a fight out of the move were the shopkeepers because it meant they wouldn't be able to sell their cigarettes and newspapers. Later the men who were taken backwards and forwards from Brighton to work there had a strike over whether they should be paid for their travelling time."

John Langley
Always A Layman

(1) Lancing Carriage Works, 1963.

(2) Horse Chestnut tree, Buckingham Park, site of army camp at Shoreham, First World War.

PORTSLADE

MAP GRID REF: 3B & 3C

CONVENT DISCIPLINE AT ST MARYE'S IN THE 1940S AND 1950S

"We had instructions every month about our behaviour and how to behave, and many a time the residents had to be shown up as a bad example if they broke silence, also because some of them used to run away with boys. Times seemed very Victorian then. We were punished if we did not do our work right. One of the punishments was to kneel in the middle of the dining-room, at the top of the room so that everyone could see us, for our meals. I was often one of those. I remember I used not to clean my wellingtons after a day's work on the farm. As I had been several times warned what would happen, eventually I had to spend three whole meals on my knees with the dirty wellingtons tied around my neck."

Mary Adams
Those Lost Years

CORPUS CHRISTI PROCESSIONS, UNTIL THE LATE 1960S

"Every year, from when I first came until the late 1960s we had a Corpus Christi procession from our Catholic Church in Portslade, at the corner of Vale Road and Church Road. We went in procession all up the road to the Convent grounds, and there were crowds of people lining the route. The traffic was not at all bad then and we did not need a police escort ... We wore straw hats for the procession at one time, and because we had nothing to keep them on with, if it was at all windy the hats blew off our heads all over the place amongst the crowds. We were not allowed to go out of our formation, but I suppose because I was afraid of being told off I did break ranks

(3) Grotto in honour of Our Lady of Lourdes, Emmaus grounds, 2019.

(4) Our Lady of Lourdes, Emmaus grounds, 2019.

very quickly. I darted out and grabbed the first hat I saw which more likely than not was not mine because we had our number tags inside them. To help us the crowds themselves went after the hats, and in doing so got muddled up with the ones in the procession. It was hard not to laugh it was so funny."

Mary Adams
Those Lost Years

OUTSIDE THE CONVENT, PORTSLADE 1960S

"I remember the first person I got to know when we started being allowed to go out and talk to people outside, as we became great friends. Her name was Mrs Jackson and I happened to meet her crossing the road down to Portslade Old Village. Her husband had died recently and she was crying. As I can't bear to see anybody so upset I went to her and talked to her and she told what had made her so upset. She invited me into her house for a cup of coffee and from then on we became friends, and every morning when I went down to get the nuns' paper I landed into her house for a chat and a cup of tea or coffee."

Mary Adams
Those Lost Years

PRAYERS

"Altogether there are three Mosques in Brighton and Hove and, on the festival of Eid, Hove Town Hall and Portslade Town Hall are used as venues for special prayers."

Brighton & Hove's Bangladeshi community, Bangla Brighton

(5) The Ronuk Hall, Portslade Town Hall, 2019.

A 'TALKING MACHINE' IN THE VILLAGE PUB

"... we had an instrument called a phonograph. This was the forerunner of the gramophone or what would be called today a record player. The records were cylindrical and slid onto a cylindrical drum. It was a clockwork instrument ... On one occasion I worked with a man called Ted Mears. He told me that when he was a boy his uncle was the landlord of the pub in Portslade Old Village. His uncle obtained one of these machines, which was believed to be the first one in Sussex. The human voice had never been recorded until this date, and word got round that his uncle had a 'talking machine'. People just did not believe it. It seemed too incredible to comprehend. Ted told me that on Sunday mornings men walked several miles to the village pub to hear it from themselves, as they just couldn't believe it."

Don Carter
Just One Of A Large Family

(6) Postcard showing Railway Inn on Station Road, c.1907.

(7) Door panel, Railway Inn, 2019

> "The public bar had some rather tough customers who disappeared sometimes for a few weeks."

BINGO AT PORTSLADE WORKING MEN'S CLUB

"... After a number of 'ups and downs' he and his wife ran a Bingo club at Portslade Working Men's Club, which was packed out on their twice weekly sessions, until Bingo lost its initial appeal."

Nat Gilroy
We're Not All Rothschilds!

TOUGH CUSTOMERS AT THE RAILWAY HOTEL, 1950S

"... I obtained four morning sessions at The Railway Hotel in Portslade. It was run by a very pleasant couple who I enjoyed working with. There were two bars and being close to the railway station, a bus terminus, and main shopping centre, there were always people coming in, as well as the regulars ... The public bar had some rather tough customers who disappeared sometimes for a few weeks. We guessed they were being detained at one of HM Prisons. When we saw a group of them talking very close together, we made a joke out of it and said, 'There are those who are about to go in, and those who have just come out!' They were no trouble to us behind the bar but one Saturday morning we had a police raid. Bookmakers ran their business from their own homes as there were no betting shops and they employed a man, known as a 'bookie's runner', to go round the pubs, collecting bets written on a piece of paper, and paying out winnings. This was not strictly legal but was done quite openly, though not if a policeman was in the vicinity."

Marjory Batchelor
A Life Behind Bars

THE BAD BOYS' SCHOOL

"I was once chosen to play football at the Reformatory School at Mile Oak Road in Portslade, where, being a bad boys' school, we had to put a guard on our clothes while we played."

Ernie Mason
A Working Man - A Century of Hove Memories

[The school referred to here had different names before it was closed down in 1977: Portslade Industrial School, Mile Oak School, Mile Oak Approved School, finally changing to Mile Oak Community Home in 1971.]

(8 opposite and 9 above) Statue formerly on display at Mile Oak Approved School, 2019 [The statue is now outside Foredown Tower. The wording on the statue translates as: "The Word Of God Lights The Way".]

ARRIVING AT MILE OAK APPROVED SCHOOL, 1940S

"Our journey's end was now in sight. Driving into a narrow lane at the entrance of which a house was on either side, we drove along this winding road with fields surrounding it. Suddenly the lane petered out and there before us was this huge house covered in ivy. There was a half-circular drive in front of it and the whole place was covered with flowers, trees and bushes. What this place was I couldn't even dream, but it couldn't be the school that I was going to. It was far too posh for the likes of me. Rich kids went to places like this. Leaving the car we entered this large house, and yes I had arrived. This was my new school."

Ron Piper
Take Him Away

FILM NIGHTS, SWEETS AND PUNISHMENTS AT MILE OAK APPROVED SCHOOL

"The boy to be punished had to queue up for the film and his sweet ration, the same as everyone else. Once he had reached the headmaster's wife, she would tell him, 'No sweets for you.' He would then have to go out into the corridor, and there sit on the stone floor with hands on knees in an upright position as though sitting to attention, with his back to the dining room so he could hear, but not see the film. The boy being punished may well know that he was to be so, so the point in making him go through all the queuing for sweets was just to prolong his punishment. There were occasions when the boys did not know they were to be punished, that is until they held their hands out for their sweet ration and then they would be told. This to me was the worst punishment of the two. There the boy would stand, in anticipation of sitting down to a film show with a handful of sweets, to be told right at the very last minute that he had nothing."

Ron Piper
Take Him Away

DEVIL'S DYKE AND THE DOWNS

MAP GRID REF: 1B, 1C, 2B & 2C

SHE NEVER WENT OUT WITHOUT HER GLOVES ON EVEN IN THE SUMMER

"To have a day out was a great thrill. Most of these days were spent with Granny Ward taking us by bus to Rottingdean, or by train to Devil's Dyke. Granny was a large woman with brown eyes and grey hair. She wore spectacles, smelled of lavender water and had little pouches filled with lavender which she kept amongst her clothes and handkerchiefs. She always wore a hat which was frequently retrimmed with different coloured ribbons and artificial flowers. She never went out without her gloves on even in the summer. Her shoes were kept highly polished and she always carried a black umbrella.

"I remember one very hot day all of us arriving at the Dyke Railway Station. Granny was feeling the heat so she put up her umbrella. Because she had difficulty in walking we all had to help push her up the steep hill from the station. I thought she was never going to get to the top. Our reward was an ice cream from the ice cream man on a tricycle with a little cart attached, where the ice creams were kept on blocks of ice."

Barbara Chapman
Boxing Day Baby

CATCHING THE TRAIN TO DEVIL'S DYKE

"... in my young days to go to the Devil's Dyke was a pleasure everybody looked forward to. Some went by open-topped brakes pulled by two horses, but many more by train. The train left the main Brighton to Worthing line at Aldrington Halt and following the line of what is now Amhurst Crescent, went under the Old Shoreham Road, past the present fire station and up the back of Elm Drive and Rowan Avenue and across a bridge at Hangleton Road. Hangleton Road at that time was just a country lane and used to dip down under the railway bridge. The train then continued north over another bridge where the library is now and up where Poplar Avenue is to the Dyke. At the top of Poplar Avenue the track of the railway still exists ... When Elm Drive estate was built about 1935 near the junction of the shops and Rowan Avenue, the railway company built Rowan Halt. The line was very steep and so when the train was crowded, there were two steam locomotives, one at the front to pull and the other at the back to push. The first train left Rowan Halt at 7am and ran till about 7pm."

Ernie Mason
A Working Man - A Century
Of Hove Memories

(10) Aldrington Station Platform, 2019.

(11) Site of Holland Road Halt, 2006.

PACKED LIKE SARDINES ON OUR TRIP TO THE DEVIL'S DYKE

"Our trip to the Devil's Dyke started from Brighton Station. We were packed like sardines into wooden carriages and soon began the slow journey via Holland Road and Aldrington Halts, before starting the heavy pull up the steep gradient to the Dyke Station, with views of the sea and the Downs all around us. At times the engine pulled so slowly that people could walk alongside at a steady pace and keep up with the train. A friend has told me of one Good Friday trip when the guard leapt out, after instructing the children not to touch the lever, picked a bunch of wild flowers to distribute, and leapt on again.

"The station nestled in a slight hollow where farm buildings now stand ... I have no memory of how we amused ourselves all day. The Edwardian funfairs, cableway and steep grade funicular railway on the north slope of the Dyke Hill, which my Dad used to recall so vividly, had all disappeared long ago, leaving only a small concrete base and a tangled cable-wire to mark their former site. My Dad once told me that when he was a young man, in the year of the opening of the funicular railway in 1897, he was pushed from the top of the north slope and slid to the bottom. His best suit never looked the same again."

Ruby Dunn
Moulsecoomb Days, 1922-1947

OPEN-AIR SERMONS AT DEVIL'S DYKE

"One preacher with charisma in full measure, pressed down and overflowing, was Dick Sheppard who used to hold open-air sermons up at the Devil's Dyke. The little steam train from Aldrington Halt was so overcrowded on one occasion that the engine gave up. I doubt whether I understood his sermons, but the man had a magnetic personality and a wonderful sense of fun."

Maurice Packman
The Church Round The Corner

DEVIL'S DYKE BY WAY OF PRESTON PARK, PATCHAM, SADDLESCOMBE, POYNINGS

"We enjoyed days out during our holidays. Mum would fill bottles with cold tea, and make some sandwiches and we would be gone for the day. One of our jaunts was to Devil's Dyke by way of Preston Park, Patcham, Saddlescombe, Poynings, and so to the Dyke. By the time we had only reached Preston Park we had drunk all the tea, so we refilled our bottles by a drinking fountain and horse trough which was alongside the road. On we would go to Withdean Farm and fill the bottles once more, then to the Black Lion and another filling. We would knock at the door of the Waterworks and ask to fill our bottles. Up the hill to Saddlescombe, knock at a cottage door for more refills, on to Fulking where we could help ourselves, and so on."

Daisy Noakes
The Town Beehive

(12) Drinking fountain, Preston Park, 2019.

TV – AN EARLY MODEL AT THE DEVIL'S DYKE HOTEL

"Although Logie Baird was well into inventing television in the 1930s, it was still some 20 years away for the masses. In 1938 a very flickery, early model was installed at the Devil's Dyke Hotel, about five miles outside Brighton. From what I had heard, the programmes were even worse than today. I walked with Neville, my best pal, to the Dyke to see their new wonder. We asked the manager if we could take a look. The second word of his answer was 'off'. Never mind the lack of television – my family couldn't even afford a wireless. That's why going to the pictures was so important to us."

Dave Huggins
Back Row Brighton

JACK AND JILL WINDMILLS

"It is outings (from school or not) that stick in the memory. One big day out from Stanford Road school in the 1950s was to a pleasure park near the Jack and Jill windmills, where the woods were carpeted with bluebells and a stream yielded jam jars of tadpoles. We had fun as we swung on ropes from the trees and floated paper boats down the river."

Andie Steer
Brighton Boy, A Fifties Childhood

HE KNEW WHERE THE BEST MUSHROOMS WERE TO BE FOUND

"Another side to my mother's father, a Cole from Lewes, was his love of the countryside. Taking one or more of the children with him he would walk for miles over the Downs. He knew where the best mushrooms were to be found, where to pick the tiny wild strawberries, and where the violets hid. Sales from these to local shops produced some small coins. My mother was, I am sure, right to have softened her view of him after his death, as he should be judged against his contemporaries and not against men of these easier times."

John Knight
A Ha'p'orth of Sweets

THE STEEP GRADE RAILWAY CILLIS

(clockwise from top left) (13) Devil's Dyke railway, c.1940s. (14) Railway sleepers beside the path that follows the old rail route to Devil's Dyke, 2019. (15) Devil's Dyke Hotel, 1930s. (16) Postcard showing 'The Kops', c.1930. (17) Remains of the Aerial Cableway, Devil's Dyke, 2019. (18) Postcard of the steep grade funicular railway at Devil's Dyke, c.1930s.

HOVE

MAP GRID REF: 2C, 3C & 4C

(19) Wish Park play equipment, 2019.

(20) Travelling Fair, 2019.

LORD GEORGE SANGER'S CIRCUS

"When Lord George Sanger's Circus visited Hove they used to stay in the Wish Road area, which was then all fields. They were a good crowd. They allowed us young kids to lead the horses along to the public horse troughs just along the seafront. I had a mare with a foal which used to trot alongside its mum without a halter. The circus used to have a parade through the town and back along the seafront. It really was something, with its stagecoach, clowns, horses, elephants, band, cowboys and Indians."

Ernie Mason
A Working Man - A Century
Of Hove Memories

BRONCO BUCKIE'S WILD WEST

"In those days, the coast road was just a muddy country road, with big holes in it filled with water. Wish Road was called Wish Meadow, and it was there that the circuses used to pitch – 'Bronco Buckie's Wild West, admission children 6d'. The kids used to save their pennies selling jars, rags, anything, and walk perhaps all the way from Carlton Hill or Kemptown to see it. I used to go as much as I could ..."

Bert Healey
Hard Times And Easy Terms

A FUNFARE OUT AT HOVE STATION

"Another thing we really enjoyed was when the circuses came. My goodness, I used to bob in under the canvas every chance I got. If we got copped, we used to say, 'Well let us do a job,' and they would let us do some work. The first thing I had to do, with another boy, was to carry this big bucket of water and put it down in front of the elephant. We went round to the back and twisted its tail and it gave us the bucket of water straight back. They were lovely circuses, really mammoth with hundreds of horses and everything else you can think of under the sun, and out at Hove Station they used to have funfares, with roundabouts, swings and coconut shies. Coconut shies were our main recreation. For a penny you could go on the pier and firework displays used to be given there and on the front and in the parks. There also used to be lovely horse shows along the front."

John Langley
Always A Layman

(21) Hove railway station window, 2019.

ALL GOOD CLEAN FUN!

"At the corner of Goldstone Street and the east end of Conway Street, now part of the bus garage, there used to be a piece of open ground. This became known as the fairground because at regular intervals it was visited by a travelling funfair, with all its usual amusements: swings, roundabouts and coconut shies. It used to bring a welcome bit of life to the town. You could always buy a packet of confetti which, of course, was meant just to throw over each other. However, we boys found that was a bit tame. It was much more interesting to push it down the front of girls' dresses. Of course, the girls used to pretend they did not like it, but really they enjoyed it as much as us, and nobody in the fairground minded either. All good clean fun!"

Ernie Mason
A Working Man - A Century
Of Hove Memories

GAMBLING IN JACKARSE FIELD

"At the top of Tamworth Road in Hove there is a cattle arch. At its north end there was a footpath which led up to the Old Shoreham Road. On the right side of the path were allotments, on the left side ran the railway line to the Devil's Dyke. No houses were there then and I don't know why, but this path was known as Tickle Belly Alley. At the top end of the path, after crossing the Old Shoreham Road, there was a lane which went up through fields to West Blatchington Farm, where the windmill is. One of these fields was called Jackarse Field. Every Sunday morning the local lads went there to gamble. Pontoon was the favourite game played. Somebody was always on the lookout because occasionally it was raided by the police. I don't know if anyone was caught, the lads were too quick for them. Most of my mates worked for Clarke's The Bakers on the bread vans. I used to wonder why they always had so much money to gamble with, until I found out that part of their job was to call on their customers to collect the week's bread money on Friday. They used to charge them for a loaf they had not received, because most customers did not keep a record."

Ernie Mason
A Working Man - A Century
Of Hove Memories

GIBBETS FARM WAS AT NUMBER 42 TO 46 ELM DRIVE

"A short way up the lane leading to West Blatchington Farm was another lane which went up to join the Hangleton Road (this is now Elm Drive). There was a small farm which we children knew as Gibbets Farm, so it is likely there was a gibbet here years ago. It is known that many years ago a 14-year-old postboy was robbed of the mail by two men. One named Rook was caught and was hanged and, as was the custom, his body was left hanging on a gibbet as a warning to others. Rook's mother collected his bones as they fell and buried them at Shoreham, in consecrated ground. Lord Tennyson wrote a ballad about it called Rizpah."

Ernie Mason
A Working Man - A Century
Of Hove Memories

SELLING ORANGES AT THE TOP OF THE THREE-CORNERED COPSE

"Sitting on the grass bank at the top of the three-cornered copse in Dyke Road, one old man called Charlie used to sell oranges from a wicker basket. Being on the main route from Brighton to the Devil's Dyke, it was a popular run for pub outings from Brighton. There were brakes pulled by two or more horses, carrying perhaps about 20 merry passengers. As they passed Charlie they used to give a cheer and throw him pennies. I used to pick them up for him, and for doing so he gave me an orange. I suppose it is hard for people today to understand that even an orange was a luxury for us."

Ernie Mason
A Working Man - A Century
Of Hove Memories

(22) The three-cornered copse, 2019.

(23) Orchard Road, 2019.

(24) Gibbet's Farm, Hove.

(25) Cattle arch, the Tamworth Road side, 2019.

SCRUMPING NORTH OF HOVE PARK

"When I was a boy, there were no houses on the Old Shoreham Road north of the ground from the Upper Drive to Shoreham, although the parks were there and orchards. Now there are houses in roads like Orchard Avenue. North of Hove Park there were lovely big juicy gooseberries like small plums; they do not grow them now. I did a fair share of scrumping here. We had to keep a lookout for a man with only one arm. He lived in the farm cottage, which has now been demolished, at the north east corner of the football ground."

Ernie Mason
A Working Man - A Century Of Hove Memories

HOVE BORN AND BRED

"Apart from the war years, Grandad lived all his life in Hove. He was born, bred, and went to school in Ellen Street when much of Hove was still market gardens, orchards and fields. The entire street was demolished in the so-called 'slum clearance' of the 1960s. He started work at age 11 and carried on working for another 64 years!"

Mark Stephenson
Introduction To A Working Man - A Century Of Hove Memories

W MILES, A SUBSIDIARY OF WEST BRIGHTON ESTATE, OWNED THE AVENUES AND LAWNS ON THE SEAFRONT

"W Miles employed jobbing gardeners, landscape gardeners and tree cutters ... As driver I used to deliver their needs - tools, bedding plants and so on - and collect the garden rubbish. I used to dump this at old quarries. There were several in the town and one was off Portland Road, now Davis Park. There was one off Vale Road, now Vale Park, Portslade. We used to pay sixpence a load ... W Miles sold the nurseries at Hove and bought another, along with a large market garden, at Lancing. We used to collect the produce and bring it back to the shop for sale that same morning ... We used to go across the old wooden bridge at Shoreham. This was the main road to the west then, and the railway crossing keeper was paid sixpence as it was a toll bridge. It is now just a footpath across the river. The road back to Brighton along the seafront, being free, was sometimes used and we made a quiet sixpence for ourselves."

Ernie Mason
A Working Man - A Century Of Hove Memories

[W Miles was a greengrocer and florist on Church Road]

(26) Old Shoreham toll bridge, Shoreham-by-Sea, 2010.

(clockwise from top left) (27) Davies Park Gate, 2019. (28) Dyke Road, 2019 (29) Ellen Street, 2019. (30) Furze Hill, 2019.

> "he started to quick-step down Furze Hill, and he laughed and said, 'Do you know, I once taught Ava Gardner to dance!'"

STREET NAMES IN HOVE – PHILANTHROPISTS AND NEED

"To most people the word 'Jew' is synonymous with wealth, but this is a misconceived anachronism. Yes, there have been a number of wealthy, philanthropic Jews, who, in the last century contributed greatly to the development of Brighton and Hove, and had a wide impact on the general life of the area in local Government and trade. The first Jewish Baron, Sir Isaac Lyon Goldsmid, had the title Baron de Palmeira bestowed on him in 1848 by the Queen of Portugal. He developed Palmeira Square and Adelaide Crescent, and gave land to St John's Church in that area. Many street names in Hove are a reminder of his generosity. But today, as in any society, there are two sides to every coin. In Brighton and Hove we have a necessary thriving Jewish Welfare Board to help the many Jews in need. They support three houses which are divided into a number of sheltered flats; also the Jewish Home for the Aged in Burlington Street, Brighton, set up in 1954, which has over 70 residents – many of whom are helped by the DSS. There are several families on Income Support and Social Security, while others struggle but won't accept 'charity'. No, we certainly aren't all Rothschilds."

Leila Abrahams
We're Not All Rothschilds!

I TAUGHT AVA GARDNER TO DANCE!

"When I was 16, Mum remarried. Her new husband was reasonably religious, in contrast to Mum, who had little Jewish background. My step-father had three children, the youngest of whom was only six. He was a good man, a fruiterer, who I learned to love. At my own father's funeral, when I was 31, he was really so supportive, both physically and emotionally. He helped me to understand the prayers and ritual, and I had a far better relationship with him than with my own mother ... He later got Alzheimer's Disease, but I can remember taking him for walks. He had been a brilliant dancer in his day and had run dancing classes. Suddenly he started to quick-step down Furze Hill, and he laughed and said, 'Do you know, I once taught Ava Gardner to dance!' He died in 1992, after being married to my mother for 25 years. Mum has since remarried. She's a very attractive woman, you know! And she still lives in the same place in Furze Hill, Hove."

Corinne Silver
We're Not All Rothschilds!

A BANGLADESHI MUSLIM WEDDING IN HOVE

"A Bangladeshi wedding has three main events. In England these events are stretched over three weekends so that it's easy for everyone to attend. First there is the Henna day, when the bride's hands are covered with beautiful henna decorations. Second there is the wedding day, arranged and paid for by the bride's parents or older brothers. Finally there comes the Walima, which is hosted by the groom's side of the family ...

"My sister's wedding took place in August 2000. A Bangladeshi Muslim wedding is loud, colourful, fun-filled and exciting. It is an event that is thoroughly enjoyed by the young and the old and it is full of traditional food and ceremony – enough to satisfy the greediest of appetites and with a guest list of nearly a thousand people, this was building into a truly grand event ... Cards were printed and friends and family were all invited. The venue was the Grand Hall at Hove Town Hall for the wedding. A traditional bridal swing stage was added to make the place complete. But what all the women and girls long for is the henna ceremony that takes place before the wedding. There is music and dance and, in our family, a good old foam, colour and silly string fight!

"Our relatives from New York arrived a month before the wedding and everyone got together to help us to make the big day flawless. Every day at my house the girls practised their dancing for the henna day. The noise they made as they danced to the Indian music was mind blowing. Luckily, I have good neighbours who didn't mind at all."

Brighton & Hove's Bangladeshi community, Bangla Brighton

(31) Hove Town Hall, 2019.

FLIRTING FROM THE BUS

"Harriet went to work on the buses. I lived in Church Road, Hove, and there was a bus stop just facing the kitchen window and she'd phone me up and she'd say, 'I'm passing by at such and such a time, watch out for me.' And she'd pass by and suddenly the back door of the bus would fly open. She'd be there, waving away. Couldn't believe it! And, of course, everybody on the bus would be looking. Ah dear, it was so funny. And I'd be hiding behind the curtains."

Aileen
Daring Hearts

(32) Behind the curtains,
The Marlborough Theatre, 2019.

CAMPING ON THE GOLF COURSE

"We used to come to Brighton, this was one of the things that Kenric used to do at the weekends, the whole group ... We said, 'Well, we're going down to Brighton and we're going to camp out for the weekend. Anybody want to come?' And all these various other people said, 'Yes! Yes!' And we would all come down here and we'd all bring our tents, and all the people who hadn't got tents would sleep in their cars. We found a good parking spot for camping on the road from the top of Dyke Road Avenue, Hove Golf Course is up there, and there was a big space of green between the road and the golf course. And we pulled off and we used to pitch our tents up there. And that was great ... we used to spend the day – we'd come down on the Saturday, go to St Dunstan's, sit out on the grass and eat our picnics and sunbathe. I suppose we had a wash somewhere, perhaps we had a wash and a brush-up at the pier, I don't know, but we found out about this Variety Club and we got ourselves in there. There's now a school in Middle Street. And they had a room downstairs with a roulette wheel, and I liked a bit of a gamble, so we went in there, and we would have a drink, a whole crowd of us, about 15, and we'd play the roulette game and when we'd had enough we'd go back to our tents and we'd light a fire and we'd go round the golf course, and any wooden posts we'd pull them all up, we put them all on the fire, and we'd sit round this fire, it's a wonder the police never came round, and we'd have a sing-song. And then we'd douse the fire and get in our tents."

Margaret
Daring Hearts

VISITS TO THE MUSEUM

"A favourite walk on Saturday mornings was a visit to Booth Bird Museum in Dyke Road, which is still there and has become very well known. There was a uniformed man in attendance, and as we were only allowed to talk in whispers, we never stayed very long."

Marjory Batchelor
A Life Behind Bars

(33) Great Black-Backed Gulls, Booth Museum, 2019.

"He would appear with a huge bagful of sweets and would throw handfuls over the grass and let us scramble for them"

WATCHING THE COWS BEING MILKED

"Further up on the left of Dyke Road was Holes Farm where they kept a dairy herd and delivered milk locally. We used to watch the cows being milked in the sheds. There were also pigs of various sizes in sties, farm horses, and chickens running around. There was quite a lot to interest us."

Marjory Batchelor
A Life Behind Bars

WE WERE AMAZED WHEN HE HIT 100 MPH DOWN NUNNERY HILL

"My brother and I waited there (Hove Town Hall) for a bus up to Dyke Road after swimming with Shiverers Club at the Old King Alfred. By this time, we'd moved to Withdean. Sometimes the President of the club would chauffeur me and my brother if our dad was too ill to come with us. We dared him once to show us how fast his huge Austin Princess would go (we must have been eight or nine at the time). We were amazed when he hit 100 mph down Nunnery Hill (The Upper Drive)."

Andie Steer
Brighton Boy, A Fifties Childhood

DYKE ROAD ... WE ALWAYS THOUGHT THAT WAS HYSTERICAL!

"We must have known the word dyke, actually, because we lived in Dyke Road and we always thought that was hysterical. So the word 'dyke' was familiar but we didn't really associate it with ourselves. It was something that American lesbians were called."

Sandie
Daring Hearts

GAS LAMPS ON DYKE ROAD

"I was born in 1946 so I remember the lamplighter zigzagging up the top of Dyke Road on his bicycle, with a pole to pull down the catches on the gas lamps. Perhaps it was because the top of Dyke Road was partly undeveloped in 1950-1955 that the gas lights had been left, awaiting a change to electric."

Andie Steer
Brighton Boy, A Fifties Childhood

PENNY'S FIELD AND MR MAGNUS VOLK

"Behind Highcroft Villas there was a field, known as Penny's [sic] Field. I think it belonged to Mr Magnus Volk, who owned Volk's Railway, which still runs from the Palace Pier to the Marina. I remember him as a kindly gentleman with very white hair. He used to allow the children from Sunday School to go to Penny's Field for an afternoon in the summer, supervised by the teachers of course. He would appear with a huge bagful of sweets and would throw handfuls over the grass and let us scramble for them. He was very popular!"

Marjory Batchelor
A Life Behind Bars

(34) Magnus Volk, c.1890s.

SUMMER OUTING BY HORSE AND CART

"... when we were children (aged between five and 14) those of us who lived around and about the Queen's Park area went to a Sunday School, situated in Islingword Road and called the Islingword Road Mission Hall (it's still here and going strong). Well, if we all attended very regularly we were given a summer treat. Here is the story.

"Down Islingword Road on the right there was a coal yard and the owner, a Mr Hawkins, had three horses and three coal carts. On the day of our summer treat, he used to polish up the three sets of harness and scrub and wash down his three coal carts, blacken the horses' hooves, and then make his way up to the Mission Hall ... About 40 to 45 children would get up into these three carts. When everyone was settled and our mums had given us some spending money (which they could ill afford) there was a good wave, a kiss from them and away the horses would plod, down Islingword Road, across to Union Road, up Ditchling Road, down Viaduct Road, along Preston Road, up Dyke Road Drive and then into a large house in Dyke Road called Pennies [sic] Field which belonged to a kind-hearted lady and gentleman.

"Out of the carts we'd scramble, into some lovely large gardens and lawns. Here we would have running races, egg-and-spoon and sack races. There were coconut shies and stalls to buy sweets and fruit (all very cheap for us poor children). At about 4pm a bell would toll telling us children that it was tea-time and weren't we excited to see these long tables laid out with bread and margarine, cakes and jellies, etc! The Minister would call hush, say grace and away we tucked into whatever we could eat, also waited on, with mugs of tea, etc. The time soon came to return home, so up into the carts we got and back home, the same way we had come, feeling quite proud with the horses plodding along and arriving back at the Mission Hall tired and excited to see our Mums again."

Albert Paul
Poverty - Hardship But Happiness

WITHDEAN AND PATCHAM

MAP GRID REF: 2D & 3D

CHILDHOOD GAMES IN CHERRY WOODS, WITHDEAN

"We practically lived in those woods as children. The big thing was camouflaged tree houses from which you could rain down imaginary boiling oil on the besieging armies; and of course we had catapults, spears and bows and arrows. We rediscovered the Stone Age with our arrows – flint – tipped and sparrow-feathered. This must have been about the time of the Davy Crockett coonskin-cap craze. Small things amused us endlessly. One was a criss-cross of balsa, fixed at the centre with a rubber-band which would gyrate in the air and return to your hand. It led us on to all kinds of experiments with boomerang and bolas. We were already adept at the lasso. I do not think we ever used these as weapons but they were nestling there in our tree-houses as deterrents if rival groups dared to encroach on our territory."

Andie Steer
Brighton Boy, A Fifties Childhood

RITUAL REQUIREMENTS OF DIFFERENT RELIGIONS AND THE CHATTRI MEMORIAL, FIRST WORLD WAR

"Very careful preparations were made to ensure that the ritual requirements of the different religions, practised by the various communities among the Indian soldiers, could be met ... At the Pavilion there were nine kitchens, generally located in huts on the lawns, providing separate cooking and washing up facilities for the Muslims, for meat-eating Hindus and for vegetarians. Special arrangements had to be made for the ritual killing and storing of the meat. There were separate bathing houses and latrines, and separate mortuaries. Hindus and Sikhs who died were cremated on the Downs near Patcham, on the site now occupied by the Chattri, an Indian memorial to the dead. Their ashes were scattered on the sea. In fact there were only 32 deaths in the Pavilion hospital, but it has to be remembered that many of the more seriously wounded did not survive the agonising journey to England."

Joyce Collins
Blighty Brighton

(35) Dedication of the Indian Chattri by HRH the Prince of Wales on the Downs, Feb 1921.

BLACKBERRY PICKING ON SWEET HILL

"The social life was good in Ashton Street. We used to go blackberry picking at Patcham on Sweet Hill off the London Road, get a big basket full, then go down to the open market and they'd buy them off you."

Alan Jeal
Back Street Brighton

(36) Fruit for sale at Brighton Open Market, 2019.

(37) Withdean Woods, 2019.

PRESTON PARK

MAP GRID REF: 3D

KING GEORGE V CORONATION CELEBRATED IN PRESTON PARK

"... in 1911 King George V had his coronation, all the schools in Brighton dressed in their school colours and marched to Preston Park to celebrate; the hot water for the tea was boiled in a steam engine, it tasted smoky. We had paper bags of buns and cakes, and a china coronation mug to keep. I was pleased to take mine home and used it for tea."

Hilda Barber
Blighty Brighton

TINY TOTAL-ABSTAINERS

"On a fine Saturday in midsummer, thousands of tiny Total-Abstainers would gather on the Level at the bottom of Ditchling Road. They represented Band of Hope groups from all the local districts, and to each group was allocated a horse and cart, or dray thing, upon which to display a tableau illustrating the battle against the evil of drink. Connaught Institute (us) decided to depict the Demon Drink being slain by the Good Knight of abstinence. Choosing someone to play the Knight may well have caused the selectors a problem but when it came to casting anything in the way of a demon, our Teddy seemed to be the natural choice, no contest really, and he accepted the honour ... simply because playing the part would relieve him of the need to walk all the way like the rest of us poor little devils ... From the Level, down Viaduct Road, across Preston Circus and along Preston Road we traipsed, and into the gates of Preston Park, each group shepherded by a few adult workers and following their own horse and cart, quite a walk for legs with an average length of 18 inches or so. And there was our Teddy, wrapped up in some red creation that had been cobbled together by one of the lady workers to make him look like a demon dragon, grinning all over his face because he was riding all the way in exchange for being slain by a wooden sword every hundred yards or so."

Sid Manville
Everything Seems Smaller - A Brighton Boyhood Between The Wars

---

PLAYING POLO IN PRESTON PARK

"I spent many years visiting Preston Park. My earliest recollection was the jubilee of King George V, when I was given a commemorative mug. Polo used to be played in the park and I can remember the horses coming very close to where we were standing. They seemed very large and we had to move quickly out of their way as clods of earth used to fly everywhere."

Barbara Chapman
Boxing Day Baby

BICYCLE IN THE PARK

"Somehow my mother managed to obtain a second-hand bicycle for me as a reward for passing my exams. Although it was very heavy and old fashioned, I was delighted. My brother took me to Preston Park to learn to ride the bicycle, which did not take me very long. I was allowed to ride it in the park, not on the road, so I had to walk with the bicycle to the park."

Barbara Chapman
Boxing Day Baby

(38) At the entrance to Preston Park, 2019

THE STANFORDS, THE FIRST FAMILY OF BRIGHTON

"In 1914 the Stanfords of Preston Manor could be considered the first family of Brighton. The Stanfords were a typical upper class Edwardian family. Charles Thomas-Stanford had been to Oxford reading Law, before going off to South Africa to become a friend of Cecil Rhodes and make money in diamonds. Initially a Liberal, he became a Conservative-Unionist, because he was against Home Rule for Ireland and a believer in Britain's Imperial Destiny. Ellen played the Edwardian lady's role supporting her husband and a number of 'good causes'. Vere, her grandson, had the traditional education of his class, preparing him to become an officer and a gentleman. He went from a prep-boarding school to his father's old house at Eton, then on to the college for artillery officers at Woolwich. He was commissioned into the Royal Field Artillery before the start of the war."

Michael Corum
Blighty Brighton

[Ellen Stanford, Lady of the Manor, was the direct descendent of the first William Stanford (1764-1851). Her husband, Charles Thomas-Stanford, was a Justice of the Peace, a Conservative MP for Brighton, Mayor of Brighton (1911-1914), received the freedom of the town in 1925 and became a Baronet in 1929.]

ROYAL VISIT TO THE STANFORDS

"Today was a very special day for us all at Preston Manor. Princess Beatrice, Queen Victoria's youngest daughter, was visiting the Stanfords. So a great deal of food had to be prepared for the meals ... It was just before 6.30am in the morning. We were in a hurry because, even on an ordinary day, it was imperative for us to be downstairs in the kitchen on time. I was a scullery maid. My friend Winnie Harvey was a maid too. We shared an attic room in the impressive manor, aptly named The Tops by the staff. The iron bedsteads and mattresses were covered by sheets and two thin blankets. The temperature in the room was hardly different inside or outside the covers on a cold night. Anyone visiting us would have noticed right away that Winnie and I did not stand still too long after getting up on chilly winter mornings. Once, the doctor came to our room to visit Winnie, who had a bad case of the flu. He only made one comment to us about our bedroom. 'What a godforsaken little hole,' he said. Then he left."

Dorothy Fuller
Write From The Beginning

(39) Postcard showing photographic image of Preston Manor, c.1890s.
(40) Three Preston Manor servants eating apples in the garden, 1929.

(41) Washstand, service bedroom, Preston Manor, 2019.

(42) Wallpaper, service bedroom, Preston Manor, 2019.

HOLLINGBURY

MAP GRID REF: 2D

(43) Double Decker Trolley Bus
No 26 Hollingbury, at the Old Steine,
Brighton. c.1939.

(44) Foyer of the Astoria Cinema,
c.1935.

ADMISSION TO THE CIRCLE

"The whole programme started at 9am and finished at midday. Entrance was 6d for the stalls and 9d for the circle (old money, of course). My mother would give me a shilling ... to pay for entrance (6d), a Lyon's ice lolly (3d) and bus fare on the 26 trolley between St Saviour's and St Peter's (three-halfpence each way). Sometimes I'd walk and use the saved bus fares to pay for admission to the circle. The kids in the circle would often drop their ice-lolly sticks and other sticky objects on the kids below in the stalls, and I must admit to occasionally succumbing to the temptation to do the same."

Len Liechti
Back Row Brighton

WE KEPT RABBITS FOR FOOD

"We ... kept a few rabbits. To get food for them we would go to North Brighton Golf Course and beyond, to get clover and any other greens they liked. We did not treat them as pets – they were for food."

Daisy Noakes
The Town Beehive

(clockwise from top left) (45) Aerial view of Hollingbury hill fort, 1954. (46 & 47) Brighton Morris Men. [Morris Men traditionally dance at Hollingbury Castle (an Iron-age hill fort also known as Hollingbury Camp and Hollingbury hill fort) at dawn on 1 May every year.] (48) Jubilee Beacon constructed at Hollingbury hill fort, 1935. [The Beacon was erected to celebrate the Silver Jubilee of King George V.]

COLDEAN

MAP GRID REF: 2D & 2E

(49) Five men working on Beatty Avenue, Coldean estate, c.1950s.

(50) Parkside Estate, Coldean, 1940s.

"The No 13 bus turned off the Lewes Road into Coldean Lane and I knew that this was what heaven must look like"

WEEKEND AWAY IN COLDEAN

"In a huge new council estate on the edge of Brighton lots of local families were being rehoused, and because they were overcrowded in their one-bedroom flat, Uncle Frank, Auntie Emm and the cousins Douglas and Anne had been allocated a brand new three-bedroom house ... I had never seen Coldean and had very little idea what to expect, but it sounded wonderful and I couldn't wait to go ... The same little blue case that would one day feature in the midnight feast that wasn't, was now about to feature in a travel adventure. It had been packed and waiting since goodness only knows when. Two clean pairs of knickers, my library book, some knitting, a brand-new toothbrush and I was ready to 'travel' ... The No 13 bus turned off the Lewes Road into Coldean Lane and I knew that this was what heaven must look like. There were trees everywhere and each house had its own front garden and there were flowers and space and everything looked so clean and new, which of course it was. No doubt there was also dust and builders' rubble, as Auntie Emm pointed out more than once, but I was used to terraced houses, backyards and basements and I knew this was definitely heaven!

"The house itself was a revelation to me. It had garden on each side of the front gate and behind the house as well, there were two toilets, hot and cold running water and a bathroom. This last contained a beautiful new shiny white bath and matching sink! I was almost overcome. In the garden were not only grass and flowers but vegetables and a rockery which filled the space between the shed and the garden fence. The tiny little plants peeping between the huge rocks were beautiful, and imagine having so much space to spare you could build something like this in just one corner of your garden. I knew straight away that Southampton Street wasn't, after all, the best place in the world. This was quite a surprise to me at that time and I realised then that the world was a bigger place than I had thought.

"The most romantic thing about Coldean to me then was being so far from the shops. No popping to the corner store for them, it was a major expedition which I thought exciting but which Anne and Douglas found a bore. 'Will you go to the shops for me?' had a wonderful ring of adventure to it, not a bit the same as, 'Pop round Viddlers, Janis,' which was what I heard at home ... All too soon it was time for Sunday tea and then the bus ride home. My head was spinning with all I had seen and done and my one big ambition was to live in a council house at Coldean."

Janis Ravenett
Snapshots - Childhood memories
of Southampton Street

SCRUMPING IN COLDEAN

"The policemen was called Mr Hyams, and he did a wonderful job in keeping law and order, at the same time being a good friend to everyone. Now I was quite convinced that Mr Hyams was gifted with eyes at the back of his head, as well as both sides. He knew absolutely everything that went on. He seemed to be everywhere at the same time. Once, when I decided to scrump a few apples from Woolards orchard at the bottom of Coldean Lane, I squeezed through the iron railings. Being the thinnest of my friends, I was able to get through easily. I had not thought about getting out again with my jumper stuffed with green apples ... As I backed out through the railings my shoulders got stuck and a pair of strong hands tried to pull me through. I realised with horror that it was Mr Hyams. Even now I can recall the sheer panic, like electric shocks going all over my body ... Mr Hyams made me stand and eat a good many of the very green apples. They were horribly sour but I chomped my way through them, thinking that I had got away with it nicely. It was my mum that had to call out Dr Rutherford the next day for my very bad tummy ache. I never scrumped again!"

Sheila Winter
Moulsecoomb Memories

(51) Shop front tiles,
All In 1 Takeaway, 2019.

MOULSECOOMB

MAP GRID REF: 2E & 3E

(52) A civic function on the Moulsecoomb housing estate at Hodshrove Road, Brighton, c.1930s.

(53) The Avenue, 2019.

THE NEW 'GARDEN SUBURB'

"The semi-detached houses were set in a valley, looking more like country cottages. Mum was a countrywoman at heart, having spent her childhood in a village. Dad thought the rent was very high, but there were three nice bedrooms, and a big garden, and lighting and cooking was by electricity, which was the very latest fashion. So Mum tried a little persuasion, offering to help with expenses by earning money at home, if he would agree to take them away from the terrible family upstairs. Their name was added to the waiting list, and they moved into 8 The Avenue in the summer of 1922 ... Despite his initial hesitation, my Dad was always pleased and proud to be living in Moulsecoomb in those early days. He used to tell our visiting relatives of the advantages of our new environment, while Mum would show her modern electric cooker and shiny copper kettle. Dad was proud of his work on the garden, and it became his chief hobby. I remember the fruit bushes and trees, and the harvests of black, red, and white currants, the gooseberries, blackberries, loganberries and apples. The front garden was always ablaze with colour in the summer, and one year Dad won a prize in the Annual Gardeners' Competition."

Ruby Dunn
Moulsecoomb Days

WOULD YOU LIKE TO SWAP?

"My first acquaintance with Moulsecoomb was in 1922, when as an infant of 18 months, I was wheeled in my pram to No 8 The Avenue, which was then a newly built house among builder's rubble, at the entrance to a beautiful Downland valley. My family loved it there, in the heart of the countryside. It was not long before I was old enough to enjoy the delights of playing on the wide green facing our house, or walking with my big sisters up to the head of the valley, to pick the wild scabious and poppies, or to play hide-and-seek among the corn stooks. I remember sitting on our wooden garden gate, when very small, and watching the ploughman with his horse, working on the land where Upper Bevendean now stands. I remember in my pre-school years, pushing my doll in her pram round and round the grass paths in our front garden, when friendly Mr Vic Taylor, pushing his baby Sheila in her pram, looked over the gate saying, 'Would you like to swap?'"

Ruby Dunn
Moulscoomb Days

RURAL BEAUTY OF THE EARLY MOULSECOOMB ESTATES

"These early Moulsecoomb estates had one great advantage, the rural beauty of their setting. South Moulsecoomb and Bevendean were contained within the base and hillslopes of a lovely downland valley. North Moulsecoomb was surrounded by farm and woodland, with an equally lovely valley to play in, the Wild Park, which we called the giant's foot because of its shape ... The narrow Lewes Road, linking South to North Moulsecoomb, was lined on the western side by the grounds of Moulsecoomb Place, followed by the fruit orchards belonging to Mr Bates which stretched almost to the railway viaduct by the Wild Park entrance. Proceeding north from the Wild Park, the western side of Lewes Road was given over to market gardens belonging to Mr Woolard. When Brighton Council bought the land, many of his beautiful rare shrubs and trees formed the basis of the landscaping we see today, stretching as far as Coldean Lane, which was truly a country lane leading to West's Farm."

Sheila Winter
Moulsecoomb Memories

COWS AND SHEEP CAME INTO THE GARDEN

"I was born at my grandmother's house, No 30 Nesbitt Road, Brighton, the first of my parents' three sons. I spent my young life living on the wonderful new estate at No 9 Manton Road, Moulsecoomb. We were the first family to live in this house, in this very rural location with cows and sheep entering our vegetable garden on many occasions, much to Dad's annoyance ... We were a working-class family, with the emphasis on the working. Most of my parents' spare time was spent making a better life for us; my dad providing homegrown vegetables, and mum making and mending clothes to help out with the budget. I never did like the knitted bathing costumes she made and even had to suffer the indignity of having my photograph taken wearing one, with my brother Stan."

Michael and Leslie Wilson
A Far Cry From A White Apron

MORE RURAL THAN SUBURBAN IN THE 1920S

"Life in South Moulsecoomb in the 1920s was still more rural than suburban. I was told at school that the name of our Estate was derived from the name of the original owner of the land, and was once Mull's Coomb or Valley. Where our houses stood there had once been a pig farm, and everything Dad planted grew well. Moulsecoomb Place, the old manor house, part Elizabethan with a Georgian front, stood back off the Lewes Road, at the entrance to our valley whose slopes were covered in cornfields. Sheep grazed at the head of the valley where the land rose towards Bevendean Farm."

Ruby Dunn
Moulscoomb Days

FRUIT FARMS, NURSERIES AND WILD PARK

"All the land on the west side of Lewes Road, between Moulsecoomb Place and Coldean Lane, was given over to fruit farms and nurseries, some of which belonged to Mr Bates and some to Mr Woollard. I remember the time when I was told that I was old enough to be allowed to cross Lewes Road on my own and walk to Bates Nursery to buy the fruit for our family. The scent of the stored fruit as I entered the wooden sheds, and watching the windfall apples and pears piled high in the wooden bushel measure, is with me still. There were also damsons and plums to be selected for Mum's annual jam-making and fruit-bottling ...

"In August and September we picked fruit in the Wild Park. The blackberries were for pies and jam and the elderberries for homemade wine. We three girls spent hours away from home, exploring the Wild Park. It really lived up to its name then; there were no fields in the valley, or Sports Pavilion. A park-keeper had a hut among the bushes, and once he let his huge black and brown dog out. It leapt up at me, knocking me flying and sending me bowling down the hillside. I have been wary of large black and brown dogs ever since."

Ruby Dunn
Moulsecoomb Days

WINE-MAKING, JAM-MAKING AND WREATHS OF WILD HONEYSUCKLE

"In August our picnics took on a more purposeful air, as we were expected to fill the empty picnic baskets with dandelions, elderberries, or blackberries, in preparation for Mum's wine-making and jam-making.

I hated these trips when I was small, as I was left strapped in the pram and told I was minding the picnic, while the family, so it seemed, disappeared in the bushes forever. I became frantic and used to shout 'Coo-ee' continually, waiting for an answering cry. When my sisters grew up and had their own interests, Dad went off on his blackberrying trips alone, sometimes as far as Mary Farm. He would be gone all day, returning in triumph with his two wicker shopping baskets laden with black juicy fruit, and decorated with wreaths of wild honeysuckle."

Ruby Dunn
Moulsecoomb Days

(54) Buttercup (Ranunculus), picked and pressed, May 2019.

AMONG THE MOST IMAGINATIVELY LAID OUT HOUSING SCHEMES IN THE COUNTRY

"The Bishop of Chichester wrote in 1939 in the preface to a pamphlet, Rents in Moulsecoomb: 'Everybody who goes along the Lewes Road must admire the appearance of the three Moulsecoomb housing estates; the layout and the style of building. Externally they do credit to Brighton Corporation and to the architects, surveyors and builders who brought it into being.' There was at this time (1920s) an enormous amount of commercial building development especially at Patcham, Ovingdean, Woodingdean and Rottingdean, but the standard of design and layout of these houses was in general far below that of the municipally planned estates. In some areas of private speculative development not one house appeared to have been designed by an architect. On the other hand, the Corporation's housing estates at North and South Moulsecoomb were among the most imaginatively laid out housing schemes in the country, ranking almost equal with the famous garden cities of Letchworth and Welwyn."

Lucy Noakes
Blighty Brighton

OUR 'GARDEN SUBURB' NEIGHBOURS

"Our neighbours in The Avenue were such interesting people, and some of them I have kept in touch with to this day. My dad used to enjoy talking to them, because they came from different walks of life and few of them were Brightonians. So great had been the publicity for this new Garden Suburb that advertisements appeared in the London Press. At a time when new houses were in such short supply, people were prepared to move into them from other towns, and some of the menfolk living in The Avenue were commuting to London.

"Across the wide green lived Mr and Mrs Meiklejohn with Jean and Munro. They owned Dalton's Bathing Station, and also ran the Amusement Arcade on the Palace Pier ... Next door to them lived another Scottish couple named Mr and Mrs McEwen who had no children and didn't like cats either. In the days before the Walls Ice Cream 'Stop Me and Buy One' tricycles appeared, they used to drive a smart van round our estate, selling halfpenny ice-cream cones and penny wafers. The wife perched in the back of the van, appeared a formidable figure to me, especially after one memorable day, when the van stopped outside our gate, and she shouted to me, 'Have yer got a yeller cat?' Thinking of my beloved ginger tom I nodded my head. 'If he gets in my winder again I'll kill 'im,' she threatened. Some years after, when my cat did in fact die, I was convinced that I knew the killer."

Ruby Dunn
Moulsecoomb Days

THE BAKER AND THE MILKMAN

"Despite our feelings of isolation, the baker and the milkman called daily at our doors. In the early days, Howard Barling and his brother started a milk round with a little cart and a churn, with brass pint and half-pint measures hanging on the side ... Then Mr Riches, a dairyman, came to live in Hillside with his wife and children, Morton and Joan, who were school contemporaries of mine. His round operated for many years, until the demands of modern hygiene made the Co-operative Dairy, with its bottled pasteurised milk, more popular."

Ruby Dunn
Moulsecoomb Days

> "We all joined the Church as it was the only recreational facility available outside the home, that is all except my dad who described himself as a freethinker"

THE ONLY RECREATIONAL FACILITY

"The first attempts at community life were centred around a wooden hut with a tin roof, in Hillside, which served as Church, Village Hall and Sunday School. First Mr Hurd, then the Reverend Carpenter were in charge of our welfare. We all joined the Church as it was the only recreational facility available outside the home, that is all except my dad who described himself as a freethinker, having broken away in his teens from the demands of a strict Baptist upbringing ... Later, more recreational facilities were provided at Moulsecoomb Place, when a Men's Club was opened, and much later a small branch library. Money was too short for Dad to join in any social activities. Good schooling for his girls was his priority, so when Irene won a Hedgecock Scholarship soon after we moved to The Avenue; there was the expense of school uniform to consider."

Ruby Dunn
Moulsecoomb Days

A PLACE FOR CELEBRATIONS

"With the growth of the North Moulsecoomb Estate from 1926 to 1930, the tin hut became inadequate, and it was a great pleasure to have a new brick building, St George's Hall, built in North Moulsecoomb. This was due mainly to pressure from Moulsecoomb Ratepayers' Association headed by two worthy local men, Mr Kilner and Mr Bankes. Now the church had two venues for its various functions, including services, for which the hall had been consecrated. At the same time Moulsecoomb Junior & Infants School had been built, with its fine stretch of playing fields running down to the Lewes Road. Both hall and fields could be hired for social functions; and this meant the main church events such as the May Queen Celebrations and the Summer Fete, with its competitive races and sideshows, tended to centre around St George's Hall as it was adjacent to the school field. By 1931 a large section of these fields was lost, by the building of Moulsecoomb Secondary School."

Ruby Dunn
Moulsecoomb Days

(55) Chairs, St Andrew's Church, 2019.

(56) Electric organ, St Andrew's Church, 2019.

(57) Door handles, St Andrew's Church, 2019.

THE UPS AND DOWNS OF MOVING OUT FROM THE CENTRE OF TOWN TO MOULSECOOMB

"My mother moved out in 1958, as a result of the slum clearance. She was moved to Moulsecoomb. She hated it there because she had none of her old neighbours with her, they were all moved to different areas. Everyone wanted to move because the houses which most people rented were bad, and the majority were moved to council property. The house in Moulsecoomb was much nicer, but my mother missed all her friends. In the war years the association was so close; they looked after each other and checked if you were okay. If you needed a doctor, someone would make sure you had a shilling to pay the doctor ...

"My father was quite happy to move, but, like my mother, he missed the people he knew ... My mother used to say about Moulsecoomb, 'You could die out here and no one would know.' My mother got Moulsecoomb and my aunt, who lived opposite, got Woodingdean. They weren't kept together; they didn't put any thought into it at all. It may have depended on the number of children you had and the size of the house you needed."

Mrs Jackson
Back Street Brighton

POPULATION EXPLOSION

"With this population explosion, tiny St Andrew's Church became quite inadequate, so the tin hut was pulled down, and on the site between it and the church, a fine new brick and stone church was built in the 1930s, with an adjoining vicarage. Keir Hett of Ardingly, Sussex, was the architect, and it is a fine tribute to him. The former church, minus its spire, now became our parish hall. We were justly proud of our new light and airy church, with its modern seating and simple altar, screened on each side by blue curtains. It was a functional building, for the curtains could be used to screen the altar completely, and the raised chancel could be used as a stage for drama productions. This phenomenon in church building is now accepted as the norm, but it was the first of its kind in this area."

Ruby Dunn
Moulsecoomb Days

MOULSECOOMB SCHOOL - NO GOOD GETTING OLD IF YOU DON'T GET ARTFUL

"... I was certain that I would find my work more enjoyable than at Whitehawk. I would make the most of the school's rural setting and develop the children's interest in nature. This elation was short-lived when I was confronted with one empty cupboard, and a few moth-eaten piles of textbooks in the other. I made do with rough paper in place of exercise books, and sheets of old newspaper for artwork, until one memorable day when I was called into the empty classroom of Miss Hemsworth, one of the elderly members of staff. She must have liked me for some reason, because, shaking her bunch of keys like a chatelaine, she unlocked and revealed a cupboard full of pre-war stock from top to bottom. My eyes opened wide to see top quality art and pastel paper, crayons, paints, squirrel-hair brushes, and exercise books. 'Where did this come from?' I asked as she loaded my arms with gold dust. 'Ah,' she replied with a smile and a wink, 'It's no good getting old if you don't get artful.' That phrase has now become a household saying."

Ruby Dunn
Moulsecoomb Days

CHILDREN WALK MILES TO THEIR SCHOOLS

"On the east side of the Lewes Road, there were no buildings beyond the end of The Highway. There was farmland where the schools now stand. Up at the top of The Avenue, when the builders' rubble was finally replaced by a landscaped green, with shrubs and small trees at each corner, some tennis-courts were laid out for the use of the residents. After Colbourne and Southall Avenues, The Crescent and Hillside were added to the estate, the numbers of children rapidly increased. We lived there with no play-parks, no schools, no church, no community centre. The children walked miles to their schools. My sisters were allowed to continue at their former Junior School, Ditchling Road, now called The Downs. Other children were placed in Coombe Road School. Some children who had moved here from outside Brighton were even less fortunate. As local schools became overcrowded, they had to walk to Falmer Village School. There were no school meals provided.

Usually the children were sent home in the dinner hour and the school gates were often locked between 12 noon and 2pm. My sisters had to carry their lunch to school, and then at dinnertime walk to a relative's house in Crescent Road, who allowed them to eat in her kitchen."

Ruby Dunn
Moulsecoomb Days

LEARNING TO READ

"Attempting to teach him to read was the most frustrating task of my young career, not encouraged by the fact that Jimmy's mum came to see me to tell me that if teaching to read caused all this upset, she would rather the lad did not learn to read at all. After all, his dad couldn't read, and he was getting along all right. I discovered later that he belonged to a family of gypsies who had been housed at East Moulsecoomb for the war period in order to qualify for civilian ration cards."

Ruby Dunn
Moulsecoomb Days

"Most of all they missed their friends; although they kept in contact, they were often far away."

SAVING HER PENNY FARE

"For Irene there was an even longer walk to York Place each day, as there were no buses running to Brighton. York Place was the site of the original Grammar School before moving to Varndean, Ditchling Road. Our only transport was a tram which ran from the barracks, the terminus being near where the present transport depot stands. But my sister usually walked, to save her penny fare. Four years later, Kathleen, my second sister, moved from Ditchling Road, to Balfour Road Senior Girls' School, so she had an even longer walk to school."

Ruby Dunn
Moulsecoomb Days

THE LAST BUS HOME

"My brother and sister were very pleased when they moved, but when they were living in Moulsecoomb they couldn't walk home, they suddenly had to remember to get the last bus. They missed being in the centre of the city. Most of all they missed their friends; although they kept in contact, they were often far away. My sister used to say it was always a nuisance; if you went to the Regent dancing, you couldn't walk home anymore – you had to get the last bus."

Mrs Jackson
Back Street Brighton

(58) Interior of Moulsecoomb branch library, c.1960.

(59) Moulsecoomb Library, 2019.

HOLLINGDEAN

MAP GRID REF: 3D

(60) Hollingdean Depot, late 19th century.

(61) Pigs on display at the Kitchen Waste Campaign at the Royal Pavilion, 11 July 1942.

THE 'PIG BINS'

"The Council supplied 'pig bins', two or three per street. This was collected and processed at the Corporation Depot Hollingdean, which gave out a sickly smell of cabbage leaves, potato peelings, etc."

Georgiana Lally
Brighton Behind The Front

PIGSWILL COLLECTIONS

"A job came in; we were told to report to the Hollingdean Council Depot in Ditchling Road, the site of which is now a block of flats. Any swill collected had to go to Hollingdean and be processed in a huge boiler."

Tim Wren
Flying Sparks

MOVING TO HOLLINGDEAN

"My gran felt terrible about moving from Ashton Street to Hollingdean. She was always moaning, 'I'm going to die in this new house, I know.' I left Ashton Street in 1956 to join the army and the family moved out in about 1957."

Alan Jeal
Back Street Brighton

JOE MAGUIRE'S JUNKYARD

"We made boats that sank. We made kites that didn't fly and we made four wheelers that seldom clocked up more than half a mile before falling to bits. But we made 'em and we did it ourselves. It is quite true that we bought our spinning-tops for a penny or a ha'penny (according to model) and it is also true that the smaller kids had to renew their stocks of marbles (12 a penny) quite often. Our marbles were the painted clay kind with a short life-span. They did not take kindly to being trodden on, and those that survived this fate soon found a home in the marble bags of the big, cocky yobs, to whom the little 'uns quickly fell victim in fair or foul play. That is why it was always the little 'uns who had to replenish their stocks. Yes, marbles and tops could be bought at the local sweet shop. If you were lucky and had tuppence to your name, you might even be able to get a rollerskate from Joe Maguire's junkyard in Hollingdean Road. Nobody ever owned more than one skate at a time. We didn't even know they came in pairs. But a skate was a proud possession..."

Sid Manville
Everything Seems Smaller

(62) Garden wall, Roedale Road, 2019.

DETOUR THROUGH HOLLINGDEAN

"My chief pal during those years was Kathleen who lived in The Highway. I was always lazy and late in the mornings so she used to come and knock on the door and entertain me during our long walk to the top of Ditchling Road with accounts of last night's radio play, or her doings at the Girls' Brigade in Lewes Road. She was more athletic than me, and I considered that she had a much more exciting life. On the way home we took a long detour through Stanmer Park Villas, via the beechwoods. We had great fun tree climbing and daring each other to do jumps. We met boys from Varndean Boys' School who chased us and left rude messages on walls. We balanced on tops of garden walls in Stanmer Villas or Roedale Road, until window-taps from irate residents sent us scurrying off. We often had the sense to stuff our hats in our satchels so that we could not be identified."

Ruby Dunn
Moulsecoomb Days

(63) Henry Soloman's gravestone in Florence Place Cemetery, 2019.

HENRY SOLOMON, FIRST CHIEF CONSTABLE, BURIED IN FLORENCE PLACE CEMETERY

"Brighton in the past, as it is today, has always been 'liberal' in its tolerance of different creeds and outlooks...the founder of the Brighton Hebrew Community was Emmanuel Hyam Cohen who came to England from Bavaria in 1782, and settled in Brighton, producing a family of ten children. Although an educated and intelligent man, on his death in 1823 he left little money. But his descendants, especially his son Levi Emmanuel and his son-in-law Henry Solomon, were the first Jews to hold posts of high responsibility in the city ... The former was founder and editor of *The Brighton Guardian* for 35 years, and the latter becoming the first Chief Constable in 1838 and holding many important inspectorates until in March 1844 he was murdered in his office by an unbalanced youth apprehended for stealing a carpet. Thousands lined the funeral route, and the murderer was publicly hanged in Horsham on 6th April 1844."

Leila Abrahams
We're Not All Rothschilds!

LOUIS GOLDBERG, THE FIRST JEWISH EMBALMER IN THE UK

"Louis was born in Stepney in 1916 during an air-raid. There was no one to help, so his mother had to deliver a breech presentation herself. It is possible that this was the cause of his spasticity. It appears that the specialist, although an honorary consultant at Hove Hospital (then a cottage hospital with 22 beds), in 1932, had little knowledge of the source of spasticity, so he operated on Louis's leg, which used to go into spasm, believing that this would help. As there were no transfusions then, he was fed on barley sugar to thicken his blood. Unfortunately an artery was cut during the operation, with the result that one leg was shortened by two and a half inches resulting in Louis, at 16, having to lie on a long, wickerwork, spinal chair ...

"At the same time, his father and his brother, Sammy, who was killed in the Battle of Britain in 1940, had taken over the premises in Trafalgar Street and were running a motor repair and engineering business. Louis, by dint of much perseverance and fed up with being an invalid, determined to take on a share of the work. Lying on his back, he would scrape the bearings, and gradually, as he became stronger, took on a more active part, so that during the war, he could not only drive, but he became a despatch rider and a mortician for the civilian dead ...

"His father, having the facilities, began contracting to the Brighton and Hove Hebrew Congregation to carry out funerals. They made the coffins and provided transport for burials at Florence Place, Ditchling Road ... In 1950 when the British Embalmer's Society was formed, Louis sat the examinations and gained top marks, thus becoming the first Jewish embalmer in the UK."

Louis and Bernie Goldberg
We're Not All Rothschilds!

ELM GROVE AND BEAR ROAD

MAP GRID REF: 3D 3E

(64) The corner of Riley Road and Bear Road, 2019.

(65) Shutters of a former shop on Bear Road, 2019.

LEMONADE POWDER BY THE HA'P'ORTH, BEAR ROAD

"A little further down the road and on the other side at the corner of Riley, was the last of the small shops in Bear Road ... it is as Kempshalls that the shop remains dear to memory, because it sold lemonade powder and raspberry powder by the ha'p'orth. What you had to do was to spoon some of this delightful stuff into a beer-bottle full of water, cork it up, give it a thundering good shake and there you had it - the ideal beverage for washing down your hunk of bread-and-marge on your day out over the hills. Mind you, it used to get a bit warmed up on the journey, and that brought out the tang of stale beer that usually hung around the bottle, but never mind, a bread-and-marge doorstep washed down with warm raspberryade is something everyone ought to have at least once in a lifetime."

Sid Manville
Our Small Corner

WOODVALE CEMETERY WAS OUR PLAYGROUND BUT WE NEVER TROD ON A GRAVE

"I have a mental picture of poor little Ivy, with one kid in some sort of pram, and with three others in tow, pushing and pulling her way up to the top of the hill and through the big iron gates into the cemetery, which was our playground. A large bottle of water and a bundle of bread-and-something were the refreshments, and flower picking, daisy-chain making and butterfly catching were the pastimes. In later years we boys would go up to the racehill to play our rougher games and to fight and whatnot, but there was something about the cemetery that made it favourite for picnicking. There was a table-thing with rollers on it, sometimes we sat on that. Yes, we liked the cemetery, the flowers were better there than on the racehill. But we never picked those on the graves, and we never trod on a grave, because Winnie said that was wicked."

Sid Manville
Everything Seems Smaller

(66) Daisy (Bellis Perennis), picked and pressed, May 2019.

IT WAS A DARK, DARK NIGHT ...

"Living opposite a cemetery was something we took for granted. Never once in my childhood days did I consider it spooky that we overlooked the dense blackness of a burial ground on dark nights, or in the outline of gravestones by moonlight. No, to us the Simbo Wall was an old friend who took an important part in our games and pranks. Most of our games were noisy but harmless - the same I'm afraid cannot be said for some of our 'larks'. One, in particular, I have always felt a bit ashamed of. It was an exceptionally dark night that two of our gang climbed over a part of the wall where they could stand on tombstones or crosses. Each of them had a flashlight torch which, shone up from below onto their faces, presented a pretty ghastly sight. There, in the darkness, they waited until someone came up the road; it happened to be a girl. With a loud, piercing scream the illuminated faces appeared over the wall, and the effect on that girl was devastating; she screamed and cried hysterically and ran out of sight around the nearest corner, and we never knew how she recovered from the shock."

Sid Manville
Everything Seems Smaller

(67) Hartington Road entrance to the Brighton & Preston Cemetery, c.1950s. [The lodge and entrance gates were completed in 1885 and are Grade II listed.]

BOOSTING FOOD PRODUCTION

"The allotments at the top of Elm Grove known as Tenantry Down were brought into being during the 1914-1918 war, with the idea of boosting food production and giving those who were able a chance to provide their family with fresh vegetables ... At one time the whole of Craven Vale, Hollingbury and Hollingdean were either covered in allotments or smallholdings. There were also allotments at Whitehawk, Patcham, Wilson's Avenue, and other sites. Four thousand allotments in the Brighton area."

Don Carter
Just One of a Large Family

A PRIZE-WINNING ALLOTMENT

"My two older brothers followed in their father's footsteps. They became good gardeners. My oldest brother won the runners-up prize for the best allotment in Brighton one year. The following year he took first prize, and the year after that the Council took his allotment for building houses. For the next two years he was so upset he didn't want to know anything about gardening, but he eventually came back to it."

Don Carter
Just One of a Large Family

COOKING SUNDAY DINNER IN THE BAKER'S OVENS

"Mr Goldring was our local baker, and like all the others he offset his heating costs by allowing the local housewives, for a modest charge, to use his ovens to bake the Sunday dinner. This was very handy for Mums with large families and small gas ovens, and for those who, especially in summer time, did not want to stoke up the old kitchen range. It was a lovely sight on a Sunday morning, to see Mums of all shapes and sizes carrying all sorts of trays covered with cloths of all colours, bobbing and shuffling down Bear Road and Newmarket Road to the Lewes Road, and disappearing down the steps of Mr Goldring's bakehouse. And there was a lovely smell for miles around when they called back later to collect. I don't know how much Mr Goldring charged for this service, but it seemed a good thing for him in as much as it kept his ovens hot for the Monday morning bake, and he probably made a little bit on top."

Sid Manville
Everything Seems Smaller

COMMUNITY SPIRIT

"In the early 1930s the various groups of allotmenteers began to form their own Allotment Societies. This enabled them to buy seeds, fertilisers and various other garden requisites in bulk and proved to be of mutual benefit to them all. It also fostered a community spirit among people with a common interest, who were able to swap information and ideas. Allotmenteers have in the main been unselfish people. A man whose cabbages were a little bit in advance would always give one to a man whose cabbages were not quite ready, knowing full well it would be returned perhaps in some other way."

Don Carter
Just One of a Large Family

(clockwise from top left) (68) Junction of Lewes Road, Bear Road and Hollingdean Road, 1930s. (69) Old Allotments in Craven Vale, c.1952. [Photo was taken prior to the construction of roads completed in 1953.] (70) Tenantry Down Allotments, 2019. (71) Lewes Road Cemetery entrance, c.1930s.

BEVENDEAN AND RACEHILL

MAP GRID REF: 3E

(72) Exterior view of the Bevendean Sanatorium, Brighton.

(73) Rest area for horse drawn funeral carriages, Brighton Extra Mural Cemetery, 2019.

(74) View from a Bevendean Garden, 2019.

BEVENDEAN HOSPITAL

"So the time passed peacefully, there were sorrows among the people, children caught fevers and the Fever Van was always carrying them to the Fever Hospital on the hill. Sadly a great many children died and we used to stand quietly watching as the small white coffins were brought out. All funerals had hearses drawn by horses, usually black ones, with black plumes on their heads."

Hilda Barber
Blighty Brighton

EXTEND AND BUILD

"The next development was in the early 1930s, when land bought from Lower Bevendean Farm was used to extend South Moulsecoomb up the valley. At the same time similar land was used by Mr Braybon to build a small private estate, Higher Bevendean, which comprised Bevendean Crescent, Medmerry Hill, Widdicombe and Nyetimber Hill."

Sheila Winter
Moulsecoomb Memories

(75) Hodshrove Farm, 1936.

A FAR CRY FROM COSY FAMILY LIFE

"... on the hilltop behind South Moulsecoomb, Mr Braybon built an estate of private houses called Higher Bevendean Estate. No sooner was this completed, than the Brighton Corporation-owned land beyond Bevendean was swarming with another estate of small semi-detached houses called East Moulsecoomb, which started being built in 1926. This Council development was part of Brighton Corporation's policy of house clearance, which proved so unsatisfactory for the uprooted Brighton families, but which was acclaimed by the Housing Department. Even less thought appeared to be given to the provision of social facilities in East Moulsecoomb. Many residents were completely disoriented, living, as it seemed, isolated in the heart of the country with Hodshrove Farm on their doorsteps. This was a far cry from the cosy family life in the backstreets of Brighton, with Gran up the road and Mum across the way."

Ruby Dunn
Moulsecoomb Days

DELIVERING BREAD BY HORSE & CART, BEVENDEAN, RACEHILL

"When we were children we used to love the job of feeding the horses in the stables. At that time Father had three horses, two were working at any one time. Each one had a break and a rest every few weeks. One was always turned out to graze over at West's Farm by the Racehill. When we used to see them in the fields and call their names they would come galloping over to us looking for titbits. Although they were working animals, it's surprising the attachment you have for them.

"Sometimes we had to walk the horses up and down Coombe Road and Riley Road when they had what we called 'the gripes'. A lump used to appear under their belly about the size of a fist and we had to keep them walking otherwise they would try and lay down. If you were to let them do that they would twist a gut, which would kill them. This did not happen very often.

"When it snowed, our horses couldn't get up the hills and over to the farms at Lower Bevendean and the Racehill; Alcorn's and West's; or to the two shops at Woodingdean who sold our bread - and we had to take as much as we could carry and walk over to them. There's us trudging up Coombe Road in a straight line walking in the footsteps of the one in front, with baskets and sacks of bread. About six of us went out taking three or four hours. We were dead beat when we arrived back to the shop."

George Grout
The Smiling Bakers

DAY AT THE RACES

"Brighton has always been what is called a 'free' course. Which means that apart from the Stand and Tattersalls Ring plus a small area known as the Silver Ring, the remainder of the course was open along the rails for the general public to enjoy a picnic 'day at the races'. And from the Silver Ring up to the half-mile post was, on race days, the domain of bob-each-way punters and the 'tanner' bookies. It was a frequent happening for some of the local housewives to hang up their tuck aprons for the day, club together for a tanner-win bet, and for a while, enjoy the thrill of a flutter. It was amusing to listen to the betting plan being whispered, 'Ere y'are gal, I'll put my thruppence to your thruppence and we'll have a tanner on Hairylegs.' Let me say here and now that the gals' favourite jockeys were Steve Donaghue and Gordon Richards. But these two always rode the favourites and you couldn't win much on them. No, a long price and a funny name were the features that always carried the gals' tanner so that a horse called Hairylegs at a price of 20-1 was a sure-fire thing. And they would boost the confidence of each other with the indisputable truth - 'Well, they've all got four legs m'dear.'"

Sid Manville
Our Small Corner

PRINCE MONOLULU - I'VE GOT A HORSE!

"Another memorable character was Prince Monolulu (I've got a horse!) in his huge feather head-dress at the Race Course. He said hello to me but I don't know whether or not he gave me a racing tip. It wouldn't have meant much to me since I barely came up to the horses' knees. All I can recall is thundering hooves and flying turf."

Andy Steer
Brighton Boy, A Fifties Childhood

BRIGHTON RACE DAYS

"The Brighton Race Days were an attraction to us when the Fair was permitted on the Racecourse. Coconut Shies, Hoopla, Roundabouts, Switch Backs, you name it, it was there, also the side shows, Boxing Booth and Freak Shows ... We had no money to spend, but enjoyed watching people spend theirs. We were not a bit interested in the Races. Every so often, one could hear hoof beats thundering by and plenty of cheering, but we turned our backs on it ...

"The walk up Elm Grove did not seem tiring. We mixed with excited people who were going up to have a flutter, but by the time we had walked around for some hours we discovered our legs were getting tired. So when the Race-goers were leaving and piling on the trams, we would wait until it was ready to go and sit on the step. The conductor was mostly hemmed in, taking fares, so we had a lift down the road. Only once did the conductor discover us and we rolled off in the road and no harm done."

Daisy Noakes
The Town Beehive

(76) Brighton Racecourse, c.1956. [View looking northwest over the 'home stretch' towards finishing post.]

(77) Main Grandstand, Brighton Racecourse, 2019.

WALKING PAST THE WORKHOUSE

"When walking down Elm Grove from the Race Course, the pavement runs by the Workhouse Wall. There would be seen a row of old ladies holding their aprons out in case some lucky punter would care to give a copper or two. A little further down the wall, the men would dangle their caps for the same purpose ... Depending on the time of day, you might also see the pony and trap, taking the toddlers back to Warren Farm School after being cared for during the day by the ladies in the Workhouse ... It seemed like the 'Haves' on the pavement, and the 'Have Nots' the other side of the wall ... The man on the gate had the unhappy task of splitting the families when they arrived. The men were sent to one block and women to another. The children were sent to Warren Farm School at Woodingdean, where they would stay till 14 years of age, then the boys were sent to work on farms and the girls put into domestic service."

Daisy Noakes
The Town Beehive

(78) The entrance of Kitchener Hospital, c.1916-1920, formerly Brighton Workhouse, built in 1865.

LUCK SPINNER STALL, RACE HILL FAIR

"There were many varieties of Lucky Spinner, the most attractive to the eye being a wonderful display of coloured lights and magnificent prizes ... Jerry was a regular at the Fair, and had the gift of the gab if ever a man did. It was chocolate and money with Jerry, and with only enough light bulbs to illuminate his stall, and not a coloured one among 'em, Jerry could hold the biggest crowd at the Fair. A tanned and handsome man, Jerry simply oozed personality, and always warmed his crowd up with a few risque jokes. He could always find among his audience a jolly, plumpish kind of woman whom he would address as 'Gal', and in no time at all would get her and the rest of his customers rolling with laughter. With the atmosphere created, Jerry would address the assembly something like this: ''Ere, I'll tell yer wot I'm gonna do,' the right hand slapped the left palm as he swiftly turned to his partner. ''Ere, Lil, 'and us up one of those specials.' Lil would stand with her arms cradling an enormous box of chocs, and Jerry, with patter running furiously, would pile on an assortment of boxes. ''Ere, not three, not four, not even five, 'ere, six boxes of the finest Swiss Chocklit assortment, and, wait a minute, 'ere I must be mad, 'ere's ten bob on top.' And Lil secured, under her chin, on top of a pile of boxes, a ten shilling note. What a prize! What wealth! We never won, but was there ever such a two penn'orth of excitement and hopeful anticipation?"

Sid Manville
Everything Seems Smaller

> "There was no reason we could think of why the 'Daughter of the Original Gypsy Rose Lee' should not flog water squirters on the side when she was not following in Mum's footsteps."

ALL THE FUN OF THE FAIR!

"'Come along Gee-arge, now's the time to get yer own back, and every one's double-loaded, berrymine.' Thus she spoke, or rather yelled, as she sat at the most remarkable sales-counter imaginable. It comprised a long draining-board-looking table, which sloped gently down to a metal-lined tank full of water. She looked remarkably like a 'Daughter of the Original Gypsy Rose Lee' who had been plying for trade at the awning of a fortune-telling tent a few hours before. But, as we said, there was no reason we could think of why the 'Daughter of the Original Gypsy Rose Lee' should not flog water squirters on the side when she was not following in Mum's footsteps. So at the draining-board she sat, calling her message to Georges everywhere. Her wares looked like toothpaste tubes in grey, zinc base looking metal, with a screw-cap at one end and open at the other. Miss Lee's assistant immersed each one in the water and double-loaded it. They only looked single loaded to us, but we thought we might be a bit too young to know the difference. A couple of deft jerks with a pair of pliers, and the fearful weapon was ready for action.

(79) Travelling Fair, 2004.

(80) Dodgems, Travelling Fair, 2019.

"As the evening wore on, the crowd became really dense, and before long it was shoulder to shoulder between the stalls and amusements. Several groups of girls, older than us, teenagers usually, giggled and screamed their way through the throng and provided George with the means by which he 'got his own back'. Armed with his double loaded squirter, and assisted by other Georges, the action was to isolate one of the girls from her mates and squirt water down the back of her blouse on top of a handful or so of confetti. This ritual was performed many times all over the fairground, and the struggles and screams were all part of the fun. What happened to the girls was exactly what they hoped would happen anyway, so no harm was done. I always had the feeling that the fun of the fair could be enjoyed so much more without what must have felt like a cold rice pudding down your back. As I said before, we were only young, and perhaps we didn't understand much about romance - ah well!

"The Fair stayed with us for the whole of Bank Holiday Week, and the lights blazed on until late on Saturday night. On Sunday it was gone. Whisked away in the night by the same magic that had brought it just a short week ago. And we were sad. But sadness was a brief and infrequent intruder into our young lives. What time for sadness? We had the sea to the South, and the countryside all around, three weeks of the school holiday left, good mates to play and fight with. What more could we ask?"

Sid Manville
Everything Seems Smaller

(81) Ghost Train, Travelling Fair, 2019.

(82) Rotor, Travelling Fair, 2019.

WHITEHAWK

MAP GRID REF: 3E & 4E

(83) Whitehawk Crescent in the 1930s, shortly after its construction.

AMONGST THE 'ELITE'

"It took many years to complete the housing programme between the two wars – the Whitehawk Estate commencing around 1930-31. Our family, consisting of Mum and Dad and seven children, were allocated one of these 'posh' houses around this time – consisting of three bedrooms, one living room, inside toilet and bathroom (this led off from the kitchen!).

"We transported our worldly goods by 'Tate & Lyle wheelbarrow express' from Albion Hill, and after several journeys of 'mudlarking' the twitten (leading from Princess Terrace to Whitehawk Crescent) we finally got settled in at No 45. We soon realised we were amongst the 'elite' as we had never seen a bath, let alone possessed one, other than the oval galvanised one in front of the fire at Albion Hill. We had to let Dad operate the 'mechanics' of using the bath, hence the reason that some people were reported to have used theirs as a coal cellar! ... The paintwork was green creosote but never mind, we were in heaven. Mum and Dad paid 11/6d. a week for rent, the remainder left from 31/6d. being for food, heating, clothing, etc."

Les McLenahan
Letter, Whitehawk Then And Now

LOSS AND REDEVELOPMENT

"In 1937, all of Whitehawk was developed along with the Whitehawk Inn and the private southern end, built by Brighton contractors TJ Braybon. The Clerk of Works (Mr Strickland) told me mum and dad that the cost of building a council house was £245 - quite a sum then.

"We had a wonderful park in East Brighton. This along with the Black Rock Swimming Pool under construction were fine venues for the community. How Brighton must miss that pool now! The war came, and Whitehawk was in the front line, bombs falling in many streets and the gasometer receiving Hitler's attentions. Our house was demolished by bombs in 1943. Ironically, at present, Whitehawk is again under redevelopment (and not before its time). It is hoped that those in charge will see that there is no poor construction this time. It is hoped the spirit of Whitehawk will always remain the same."

Les McLenahan
Letter, Whitehawk Then And Now

TERRIBLE TASK MASTERS

"Owing to the fact that during the 1914-1918 war no houses had been built ... the building trade became very busy. The Council decided to build working-class houses on various vacant sites such as Pankhurst Avenue and Queen's Park, Moulsecoomb, Whitehawk, etc. All good experienced carpenters, plasterers, bricklayers and plumbers would not work on these Council house schemes (unless we were forced to) because the various building contractors employed foremen (who wore bowler hats) who were terrible task masters and wanted one and a half day's work carried out in one day."

Albert Paul
Hard Work And No Consideration

BUILDING THE WHITEHAWK ESTATE

"I've been living on Whitehawk since 1936. I moved there from Albion Street in central Brighton. That's what the estate was built for - to rehouse people from the slum areas of Brighton. The Whitehawk estate was opened in 1934. The houses were built without subsidy, and very quickly. We've got a record of one batch of 200 houses which were built in one year; and those finished in 1933 are now mostly down. The real deterioration in the housing took place from the mid 1960s to 1970s, when the future of the whole estate was in question, and they are a lot worse today than they needed to have been. But the history of that area is that it has been ignored both in respect of social facilities and repairs, and amenities that people might expect."

Father of three, picture framer,
Brighton On The Rocks

NEW SCHEME

Since the total redevelopment of the estate was first mooted in 1968/69, the Council seemed to leave the place alone and didn't paint, didn't repair windows ... The redevelopment plan was originally to replace the 1,000 units of accommodation with 1,600 over 15 years. Six different schemes were put forward. The scheme they have opted for is approximately 50:50 municipal and Housing Association development, and the amazing thing is - when the estate is finally developed, which in view of the cuts is a very long way off - the Council will end up about 11 units better off and the rest will be Housing Association, of which the Council have a 50% nomination."

Father of three, picture framer,
Brighton On The Rocks

GARDENS WERE 'TOO BIG'

"Eight years ago, Brighton Council announced that it wanted to pull down half this estate, re-house those displaced on half the space they had formerly occupied, and let private builders develop the other half. The existing gardens, they explained, were too big, and the town was short of building land. Another protest. The Council said that the spare half would be given to Housing Associations but the destruction was to go ahead. The scheme is now frozen half way through."

QueenSpark Rates Book Group,
Brighton On The Rocks

WHITEHAWK HEADMISTRESS WAS PREPARED FOR FISTICUFFS WITH PARENTS

"In September 1941 I started my first teaching job at Whitehawk. I found it tough going, but my head teacher, Miss Brooker, was one of the best I ever had. She was also the President of the Brighton N.U.T. She was a strong healthy-looking woman, a keen swimmer, with a bluff hearty manner, who could stand up well to the threats and verbal attacks of parents. If a local mum rushed into the school with a grievance, rolling up her sleeves in anticipation of a bit of a barney, I have seen my head roll up her sleeves and face her, which usually had the effect of ensuring a reasonable discussion. I felt sympathy for those parents and their children, however difficult their behaviour, because in the isolated Downland estate, they were only suffering the same traumas as my own neighbours in North and East Moulsecoomb."

Ruby Dunn
Moulsecoomb Days

BUILDING STANLEY DEASON HIGH SCHOOL

"... looking out over the sea is Roedean Public School for girls, set in extensive grounds with fees of £3,900 a year. Further north ... on the Whitehawk Council estate ... is one of East Brighton's secondary schools, Stanley Deason High School. Or rather half of it. Its building was stopped in 1976 as the result of government cuts and the other half had to use the buildings of an old school three quarters of a mile away. The new school's sports complex was frozen for five years. As the result of the cuts there are two fewer teachers and 40 more pupils, a reduction in remedial teaching, in technical drawing and in educational visits."

QueenSpark Rates Book Group
Brighton On The Rocks

(84) Whitehawk Bus Garage, 2019.

(85) Brighton Transport: Double Decker Bus No. 3 Whitehawk.

BUS DRIVER'S MEMORIES - FRUSTRATING, SOUL-DESTROYING, BUT NEVER BORING

"When I started we had 18 No. 1s and No. 2s running out of Whitehawk Garage. We've now got something like four. The garage was crammed full. I used to look forward to work because it was different. Even today there's no way you can call it boring. It can be frustrating, soul-destroying, but never boring. There was a certain friendliness then because you were on the same routes all the time. You get to know the people and their quirks. Some talk to you and some are rude to you, and you gradually get to

know how to deal with them
all ... It becomes a part of
your life. I think the public
also regret that they don't have
the same drivers ... and of course
they had a conductor with them
too who was their mate."

QueenSpark Rates Book Group
Brighton On The Rocks

PIG FARMS

"The large Whitehawk housing
estate was in my day called
'The Piggeries' because there
was a great many small pig farms.
Several hundred pigs - and they
didn't 'arf smell! - were housed
in rusty old broken down sheds
(or rough stables, because horses
as well were kept there)."

Albert Paul
Poverty - Hardship But Happiness

HUNDREDS OF GERANIUMS AND
ASPIDISTRAS ON THE KERBS
SOAKING UP THE RAIN

"Practically every house,
although the people were poor,
was very fond of geraniums and
aspidistras. These were placed
in pots in nearly all the
windows - they did look nice.
Well, when it rained hard,
the people would put all these
potted plants out into the street,
stand them all in a row on the
kerb stone to catch the rain and
so give the plants a good soaking -
hundreds and hundreds of them
in all the streets was quite
a common site."

Albert Paul
Poverty - Hardship But Happiness

(86) Geraniums in Whitehawk, 2019.

(87) Geraniums in the window,
Sutherland Road, 2019.

(88) Geranium (Pelargonium),
picked and pressed, May 2019.

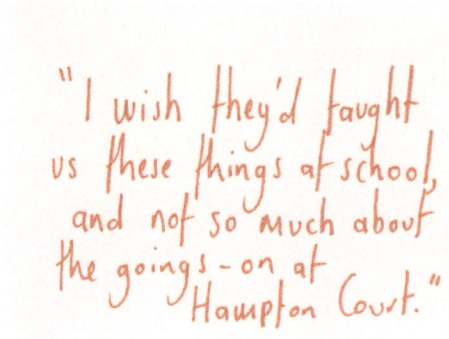

IRON AGE SETTLEMENT

"It was many years after my school days that I read in a book of local history that the area about where the Grandstand is, at the top of Whitehawk Hill, is the site of an Iron Age settlement, probably the oldest known to man - what about that then! ... I wish they'd taught us these things at school, and not so much about the goings-on at Hampton Court."

Sid Manville
Everything Seems Smaller

THE LADY OF THE VALLEY TREADS HER GHOSTLY PATH

"I can only tell the story as my grandfather told it to me and as his grandfather told it to him. The story of Whitehawk Valley and the Lady who, it is said, has been seen to walk its depths - in spirit form - when the nights are dark and wild ... Whitehawk Valley is cut deeply into the Downs on the eastern limits of Brighton and excavations in recent years prove that the district has been peopled since the Iron Age. But the Lady, they say, is arrayed in medieval style dress and as she treads her ghostly path, she carries aloft on a gloved hand, a white hawk ... None among those who have told the story down the ages can suggest who the Lady is or was. Nor do they know why, from time to time, she chooses or is compelled by some mystic force, to return to haunt the valley, but from time immemorial the valley has borne the name 'Whitehawk'."

Sid Manville
Our Small Corner

(89) Whitehawk Hill Path, 2019.

BLACK ROCK

MAP GRID REF: 4E

EXPLORING BLACK ROCK RUBBISH TIP

"The rubbish dump in those days was at Black Rock, and some of the kids used to go there to see if they could find anything ... my next adventure, or misadventure, was to go with some boys to the dump, searching the rubbish. We never found anything, only empty cocoa tins, condensed milk tins, tea packets, stale crusts, hones, fish heads and filthy hands and clothes full of coal and chalk dust. I soon packed that up; Mrs Tester had to wash all my clothes and I had to have a thorough scouring and washing, and have disinfectant put on me."

Bert Healey
Hard Times and Easy Terms

AWAY WENT THE RUBBISH DOWN INTO THE SEA

"The dustbins were supplied by the landlords to the tenants. Twice a week a horse-drawn cart would arrive at the houses. The dustmen would put a ladder up to the cart – there would be three dustmen. They would open the house doors and shout, 'Dust? Dust?' In they would go, out into the back yards, pick up the dustbins, go back through the house, up the ladder, empty the rubbish into the cart and then return again through the house with the empty bin, with the inside covered with disinfectant powder. When the dustcart was full the dustmen would trot the horse away to Black Rock (Kemptown), back the cart to the edge of the cliff, then turn a handle and up would go the cart container and away went the rubbish down into the sea. They would turn the handle again, putting the dust container back into position, and away they would go for more rubbish."

Albert Paul
Poverty - Hardship but Happiness

(90) Black Rock swimming pool, 1961.

BLACK ROCK WAS LIKE BEING IN BUTLIN'S

"The fun swimming was at Black Rock (now Brighton Marina), where there was an outdoor swimming pool with boards and outdoor table-tennis and you could go down to a 'private beach' and there were rock pools and ice-cream. It was like being in Butlin's for a day. Anyhow, I had been a habitué of the seafront since my first winter of 1946-47 when we lived by Morgan's the chemists in Arundel Road. Here my mum got round the electricity cuts by boiling-up water on the gas-ring, putting hot water bottles in my pram and running up and down the seafront. That way she kept herself warm as well. I got the feeling that Black Rock served mainly that end of town. People did not leap into cars and travel miles from Hove for their pleasures. They did not have cars, and outings like Black Rock were memorable because they were exceptional."

Andy Steer, Brighton Boy
A Fifties Childhood

BLACK ROCK BOASTED A MAGNIFICENT POOL

"When I was a child Black Rock boasted a magnificent pool with deck chairs all round the edge, and a paddling pool at one end of the enclosure. We spent many happy hours playing in the water – sometimes just we two, sometimes with friends – and the best bit was that Mum and Dad would often join in. They both enjoyed swimming and tried to teach us the art of diving as well – to no avail I'm afraid: neither Bert nor I ever got to grips with diving; an inelegant belly flop was the best we achieved – but Black Rock Pool was a Mecca to us. Sadly, it no longer exists; it was destroyed in the name of progress to make way for Brighton Marina."

Janis Ravenett
Snapshots

BLACK ROCK POOL DEMOLISHED

"On the coast to the south is an open-air swimming pool, the Black Rock pool, which served the estate and indeed all of Brighton. In 1968, 81,000 people swam there during the summer months. In 1978 it was closed, having been allowed to decay due to inadequate maintenance and blight from building works nearby. A large public meeting was held which unanimously asked for its reinstatement – with one dissenting voice, the local Tory Councillor, a hotelier who wanted the area developed as a motel. The Council has decided in favour of demolition, and asked for tenders from private leisure developers to rebuild the site."

QueenSpark Rates Book Group
Brighton on the Rocks

(91) Vacant site, Black Rock, 2019.

(92) View east from Black Rock to the Marina, 2019.

WOODINGDEAN

MAP GRID REF: 3E & 3F

(93) Woodingdean Lawn Memorial Cemetery, 2019.

LITTLE METAL BOXES

"Someone's bright idea of these prefabricated metal 'little boxes that all looked just the same', was the first home I recall and these early years were overwhelmingly happy times. Sure, there were lots of painful bits - who didn't have them? - like poverty and prejudice and parents that always checked your ears were clean before bed; but despite these minor encumbrances to childhood, it was on the whole pleasant, blissful even.

"Altogether some 250 or so identical prefabs comprised this estate of 'homes-fit-for-heroes'. Doubtless, a comfortable middle-class Civil Servant somewhere in the Ministry for Social Improvement for the Masses planned it all at Labour's behest, while seeking to further the Victorian cause of moral improvement, by adding a literary slant with place names derived from Rudyard Lockwood Kipling, no less. We had Rudyard Road and Kipling Avenue bounding our road, Lockwood Crescent ... Rudyard Kipling, like our council estate, wasn't always popular in some quarters; with his praise of ordinary folk and his anti-imperialism that ruffled feathers. He had lived at Rottingdean, close to Woodingdean, a place that I would often visit ... looking back, I wonder if I wasn't searching to be free of the uniformity and oppression generated in me by these mass-produced identical white metal boxes that all looked just the same. But as a child I knew nothing else; and as they say, a house is what you make it, and my parents made it a smashing place to live, a real home for our family: my mum, Mary, from Tipperary; my dad, Bill from over the hill - Whitehawk, that is; my Brother, Michael - 11 years older than me; and yours truly, the baby."

Keith Jago
Remember the First Time?

SELF-SUFFICIENCY

"Now, while each prefab was identical, ours had a bigger garden than most because we lived on the bend. It was enormous, maybe 100 yards long; providing playground, allotment, poultry house, rabbit hutch, garden shed; and still with sufficient lawns to keep my dad mowing endlessly. It was self-sufficiency par excellence and my dad grew the biggest vegetables you have ever seen; onions to bring tears to your eyes. We had animals in abundance: chickens, ducks, geese, rabbits, newts, lizards, slow worms and even snakes - as well as a cat and dog. This was real self-sufficiency ... that's

---

how it was then. Rationing remained, poverty was widespread, and self-sufficiency offered self-preservation and survival; and my Dad was good at it; and it gave me plenty of fun, too. For me, though, the high spot was a children's playground where I, and most of the other kids in the neighbourhood, would play contentedly, or harass the poor chickens, or something equally dastardly."

Keith Jago
Remember the First Time?

(94) Woodingdean prefab estate, 1953.

"The girls would lie in the sun and share secrets with each other, making daisy-chains and dreaming about being country children and living on a farm for ever"

OVER THE HILLS!

"'Can you come over the hills? Go and ask your Mum.' The cry seemed to fill the universe as excited children ran from house to house rounding up their friends ... Outside on the pavement stood the cause of all the excitement – Mrs Rose Thomsett – big-hipped, big-hearted mother of three and ... famous 'camper outer'. Each year during the long summer holiday she would organise two or three trips to the country for a picnic, and any child resident in the street or close by was allowed to join in ... Once the cry had gone up, children would disappear to pester their mothers for permission, bus fares and food ... The tension and excitement were almost too great to bear as the anticipation mounted. Eventually – after what seemed like years since the first cry of 'Over the hills'– everyone was ready and assembled and off we set. We were a long, straggly, untidy crocodile of street kids. The ones whose mums weren't coming carried a parcel of food and a bottle of drink. Many of the sandwiches contained nothing more exciting than jam, and often the drink was tap water in an old lemonade bottle - but who cared? FREEDOM–THE COUNTRY–TREES–WOODS–GOSH!

"The picnic place was called Woodingdean and was only about three miles away; but this was before families had cars, and not many of the children ever went so far from home. With much shouting and laughing we made our way to Elm Grove to wait for the bus that would take us to that magical place – the country ... After a journey of unbearable suspense – would this bus never go any faster? – finally, we were there among the green fields. With whoops of joy we dashed across the road and into the woods – where now is a garden of rest and a graveyard. There were no houses in sight and no hint of the huge housing estate which stands there now ... The first priority for the accompanying mums was to find a nice comfortable spot to sit down; not too hot, so it must be fairly shaded but not so shaded as to feel chilly.

"All we children dumped our food, drink and jumpers near the grown-ups and disappeared with whoops of joy to begin the real adventure of the day. Total freedom to climb trees, fight, play Cowboys and Indians - anything our hearts desired for a whole day ... The mothers now set about the serious business of their day out: a brew of tea! Of course for this they needed a fire, so some of the more biddable children who had not yet made off were set to collecting firewood. Very soon there was a lovely camp-fire blazing and the billies were boiling away ready to make tea. The women settled down for a good long chat and several cups of char, while the younger children played round about them. Through the trees could be heard the yells and whoops of the older ones ... After some time, most children drifted back to the fire to eat their sandwiches - and some managed to cadge a drink of tea. The women would produce biscuits to share round, and maybe a few sweets. Sweets were still rationed in those days ... Later, some of the girls would lie in the sun and share secrets with each other, making daisy-chains and dreaming about being country children and living on a farm forever. The boys would have tug-of-war games or build their own camp a little way away and who knows what they talked and dreamed about ...

"All too soon, it would be time to start the mammoth task of rounding up the children and their belongings to begin the long trek home. The shadows in the street would be long in the dusk as the crocodile crept slowly home. But what a day it had been, and what tales they had to tell their mums as they got ready for bed. And what a wonderful sleep they would have that night after all that fresh air and adventure!"

Janis Ravenett
Snapshots

(95) Happy Valley, Woodingdean, 2019.

Three-Cornered Leek (Allium Triquetrum), picked and pressed, May 2019.

ROTTINGDEAN

BEATING THE BOUNDS

"I cannot finish writing these memoirs without mentioning the day in 1928, when Brighton took over Rottingdean and some surrounding districts. We were all given large sticks with which we beat the bounds, having to walk all round the local hills. This is an old country custom to keep the imaginary line which separates the old parish boundaries. We ended up in the evening with very tired and sore feet."

Margaret Ward
One Camp Chair In The Living Room

SHERBET DABS AND DEAD FLIES

"In the early 1930s the bungalows in Eley Drive and Eley Crescent were built, so it was necessary to have a road leading to them from Falmer Road. This was called Court Ord Road. Before this there was just a rough grassy track leading to an old wooden shack and a field of marguerites, poppies and pink and blue cornflowers. In the old shack lived Jurry Murrell and her husband. She kept a small sweet shop, with sherbet dabs and liquorice shoelaces. In her bottles of sweets were usually some dead flies. We were told never to buy sweets from her, but quite often that would be where our Saturday pennies would go."

Margaret Ward
One Camp Chair In The Living Room

SUNDAY WALKS AND FORBIDDEN SWEETS

"When we were children, we used to go to Sunday School at 10am and then on to church at 11am. When I was very young our Sunday School teacher used to sit me on her lap for the church service. Her name was Miss Crookenden, and she did an enormous amount to help the villagers. She was also an aunt of Sir Laurence Olivier. On Sunday afternoons we went back to Sunday School at 2.30pm, after which Mother and Father would meet us if the weather was fine and take us for a walk. Father would wear his best suit and carry a very fine polished walking stick. Mother was always in her best clothes, as we were. We only wore them on Sundays and special occasions ... Sometimes they took us over the hills if it was not muddy. We would go up 'Breaky's Bottom', behind New Barn Farm, between the hills and then onto 'Honeysucks' at the top of the hill. On the horizon there were lovely gorse bushes which smelled so beautiful when in bloom. Our other favourite walk was up the Falmer Road and over into Ovingdean village, where we stopped to look at the cottage gardens. Father would explain to us about the flowers and shrubs, as he was a professional gardener, having served his apprenticeship at a large house in Esher, Surrey."

Margaret Ward
One Camp Chair In The Living Room

THE TIDAL WAVE CAME RIGHT UP TO THE MAIN ROAD

"On summer days we spent a good deal of our time on the beach, swimming, prawning and winkling. Mother used to meet us from school and we would have a picnic tea down there. There was once a tidal wave. The tide was very low at the time, and as the sky grew darker, forming a straight line above, the wave came right up to the foot of the cliff and up the slipway to the main road. Everyone ran and left their possessions on the beach. Thankfully, no-one was drowned. It was an eerie sight. I must have been about 13 years of age at the time and was very apprehensive for a long while after."

Margaret Ward
One Camp Chair In The Living Room

(97) Rottingdean, The Beach & Slipway.

SLIPWAY, LOST SAND AND CAVES IN THE CLIFFS

"The slipway led from the road down to the beach itself and was extremely slippery with green seaweed at the bottom where the sea washed over it. At the top were about four fishermen's huts where they used to mend their nets and keep their boats and tackle. They could slide their boats straight down the slipway into the sea. Granny's brother was a lobster fisherman. He was always there with his lobster pots ...
We lost the sand in the 1930s when the undercliff walk and the large concrete groynes were built from Saltdean to Black Rock. Before this the groynes were made of wood and looked much nicer. There were also caves in the cliffs, which led up to the cellars of various houses in the village. We were told not to go into these caves, but needless to say we did."

Margaret Ward
One Camp Chair In The Living Room

SCHOOL BUS CRASHES THROUGH A FLINT WALL

"We had no bus service for many years from the village up the Falmer road. It was first started by a Mr Price in the 1930s, soon after I left school. I was coming home on it one day and when we got to the top of Doctor's Hill it turned right round to the left and went right through the flint wall and into the stables which have now been converted into a house. We were all very shaken at the time; this bus was a single-decker, not very large and privately owned."

Margaret Ward
Memories of Rottingdean

THE SCHOOL BUS SLOWED DOWN TO PICK YOU UP

"When our children went to school there was a small bus, and every other one went to Woodingdean. The one in between only came to our estate, and the bus drivers took our children safely to school. The drivers' names were Joe, Dan and George. If you left it a little late to get the bus as it came down the road they would slow down and pick you up. They wouldn't dream of passing you or taking off and leaving you behind if they saw you running."

Margaret Ward
Memories of Rottingdean

RACING SILKS

"Every time Brighton Races were on, a jockey named Jimmy used to stay as a lodger with my mother and father and I well remember mother ironing his silks which were beautiful colours and the texture of the cloth was a delight to touch. He was a little man and always very happy."

Margaret Ward
Memories of Rottingdean

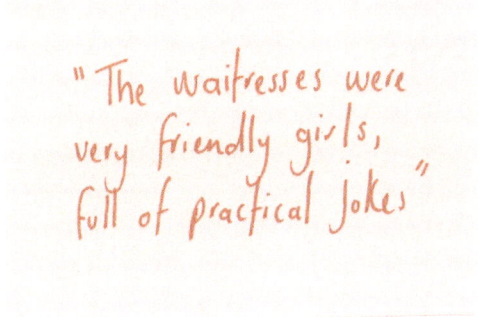

SEASONAL JOB, ROTTINGDEAN CAFÉ

"... I got myself a seasonal job in Rottingdean at a café with a shop attached. The manageress was Rose Smart, who later became a family friend. I was in charge of the shop, which sold sweets, chocolate, ice cream and minerals ... Standing in the shop, which was near the edge of the cliffs, there was plenty of fresh air and always something to see. In September, when the tides were at their highest, I had to keep the shop door closed, and the customers had to make a dash to get out between waves or risk a soaking. I learned to make sundaes for the waitresses, serve in the shop, and take bills from the customers as they came out ...

"I had never worked with waitresses before and I found them very interesting. They would slink in late for work in the mornings, looking very pale and tired, with a muttered, 'Morning. Is the boss in yet?' When they emerged a few minutes later, it was like a transformation. Careful makeup had been applied, cheeks glowed with colour, lips were bright, and with mascara separating the lashes the result was really startling. Most of them were from London for the season, returning about the end of September, combining work with the attractions of the seaside.

"The waitresses were very friendly girls, full of practical jokes, to my embarrassment at times. On a quiet afternoon at the end of the season, when it rained hard, one particular girl would come into the shop and ask if she could use the telephone. Looking through the directory, she would phone a fishmonger and ask if they had any dry fish, and if he said, 'Yes madam,' she would say, 'Bloody well give them a drink!' and hang up! Or she would find someone by the name of Smelly and ask, 'Are you smelly?' then say 'Well do something about it then!' I had to laugh, although apprehensively, as we were not allowed private phone calls. The only time I used the phone was to call one of the cooks to take the order for the next day's supplies, when the manageress was busy in the kitchen."

Marjory Batchelor
A Life Behind Bars

(98) Postcard of The Cliffs, Rottingdean, showing Tea Rooms, 1904.

(99) Shane's Kitchen, 2019.

WORKING FOR MISS BACON

"My next situation, when I was 17, was on the Rottingdean Heights, where I cooked and kept house for a Miss Bacon. She kept a high-class bookshop opposite the White Horse Hotel. She lived in a Tudor-style house with her invalid father, and my duties included looking after him as well. Here I earnt £1 per week rising to 25/-."

Margaret Ward
One Camp Chair In The Living Room

MR HILTON THE LAMPLIGHTER

"In those days all the streets were lit with gas lamps and in the early evening we would see Mr Hilton come up the road with his long pole to light them. He had to come round again in the morning to put them out and must have walked miles in a day, but always appeared to be cheerful."

Margaret Ward
One Camp Chair In The Living Room

OLD CHARLIE ENTERTAINS

"... we all loved ... Old Charlie. He was always to be found at the White Horse Hotel, where the buses turned the corner into the High Street. Charlie had shoulder-length white hair and always carried a white rat on his shoulder. He often recited Shakespeare and the passengers used to throw money to him from the top of the bus."

Margaret Ward
One Camp Chair In The Living Room

DANCES AT THE MAST HEAD

"On the cliffs to the west of the White Horse Hotel was a large house which gradually crumbled into the sea. At the front of the White Horse was a wooden hut called The Mast Head ... This was where the village dances were held and where I first started dancing. The present village hall was built in 1935 and was opened by George Robey, who used to live in the village ... The first dance I remember there was to celebrate the Silver Jubilee of King George V and Queen Mary. It began with a torchlight procession from the seafront up the High Street, round the pond and up the Hog Platt to the windmill, where there was a large bonfire. Hence the name Beacon Hill. A beacon was always lit there to celebrate any special occasion, and the torches, reflected in the pond, always looked spectacular."

Margaret Ward
One Camp Chair In The Living Room

(100) Rottingdean Terraces Stage, 2019.

THE ENDOUS CLUB

"A dozen of us got together and formed a social club which we called 'The Endous Club'. This was named after the cottage in which Bob Copper lived, because it was his idea to start the club. We used to meet in a little cottage named Satis House, at the bottom of West Street, in which Eric and Ina lived with their widowed mother. Three of the boys formed a musical trio. Bob had a bassoon, Les played the piano and Eric strummed the guitar. For a while Eric was my boyfriend, though this did not last. The same thing happened with Les. I suppose it was inevitable really, as we were together so often and held lots of parties ... We often went to dances together. We thought nothing of walking to the Peacehaven Hotel wearing very long backless evening dresses and carrying our evening shoes. If we were lucky, one of the boys would manage to get his father's car, and after the dance we would all pile in and go up to Brighton Station for hot chestnuts and coffee."

Margaret Ward
One Camp Chair In The Living Room

PICNICS, THE HILLS PAST ST DUNSTAN'S AND NANCY SPAIN

"Margaret and I used to come down to Brighton, used to come to Brighton often, come early in the morning, bring a picnic; Margaret used to make a picnic, we used to sit up on the Downs. But we never went to the clubs, Margaret and I never went to the clubs; we used to go and have a drink or bring a picnic and sit on the front, or we used to go on the hills past St Dunstan's and up on the green there - that was mostly where we went because I enjoyed being up on the hill and watching the cliffs and all that. We walked all along there, by Roedean. We used to say, 'Nancy Spain went to Roedean.' You felt a connection, you see, because you knew she was gay."

Vera
Daring Hearts

(101) Roedean School, 2019.

SALTDEAN

MAP GRID REF: 4F

(102) Saltdean Cliffs, 2019.

(103) Saltdean Undercliff, 2019.

FATHER SAVES A MAN

"He always seemed to have a story to tell. One was when he saved a man from drowning when they lived at Saltdean. This man was named Mr Chandler, and I know it to be true because his wife often used to say to me, 'It's thanks to your father that I still have a husband,' and his daughters Dorothy and Joan went to school with me."

Margaret Ward
Memories Of Rottingdean

FATHER'S FALL

"... while they lived at Saltdean he fell down the cliff and broke his leg. He was lying on the rocks below and the tide was coming in when fortunately a woman was walking on the rocks and she sent for help. He had to lie for weeks with his legs between sandbags, this was before splints or plaster were heard of. It must have been 1915 ..."

Margaret Ward
Memories Of Rottingdean

GATHERING DRIFTWOOD

"The men used a rope tethered to the cliff top to go down to get driftwood, there were no steps in those days."

Margaret Ward
Memories Of Rottingdean

THE OCEAN HOTEL AND THE LIDO, SALTDEAN.

(104) Ocean Hotel and Saltdean Lido, Saltdean, c.1938.

'Grand Ocean' luxury apartments, front terrace, 2019.

PEACEHAVEN

MAP GRID REF: 4G & 5G

NEW LIFE IN PEACEHAVEN

"With so many men returning from the war with impaired health, the 'health-giving breezes' of life upon the Downs probably held a large appeal; and many disabled ex-servicemen decided to invest their service pension in a new life in Peacehaven. A Mr Sayers, who had been gassed in the war, bought three plots of land after being advised to leave London by his doctor. According to the *Peacehaven Post* (October 1921), Peacehaven was just the place for ex-servicemen like Mr Sayers to invest their pension, and reported walks around the estate almost always included a 'chance' meeting with recuperating residents, such as 'Mr Sanderson, visibly rejuvenating', and his neighbour Mr White, disabled in the war and advised to move to a healthy spot.'"

Lucy Noakes
Blighty Brighton

FAR CRY FROM A 'GARDEN CITY BY THE SEA'

"Many of the plot holders could afford to buy plots of land but could not afford to build on them ... this resulted in many of the plots remaining vacant, eventually leaving the development with a scattered, haphazard appearance. Many plot holders who could afford to build could do so only with the cheapest materials, creating a landscape of caravans, wooden shacks and half-finished bungalows, interspaced with the grander villas which wealthier plot holders had been able to build. This shanty-town appearance was further enhanced by Neville's policy of selling plots without services, which left the town with one made-up road and the distressing lack of a sewerage system. All this was a very far cry from the 'Garden City by the Sea' which Neville had intended to build, and which he continued to advertise Peacehaven as."

Lucy Noakes
Blighty Brighton

STREET NAMES CHANGED

"Although to its inhabitants Peacehaven may have seemed the rural idyll they had been searching for, to its attackers it was one of the worst developments of the modern age; encroaching on a part of rural England which was central to ideas of Englishness, and symbolising the lack of social control and breakdown of order which seemed to typify the post-war age ... In a competition to choose a name for the new estate, New Anzac-on-Sea was chosen as the winner; but as a result of representations that Anzac was almost a sacred word, following the tragic events of Gallipoli, it was not a name which could suitably be used to advertise a new seaside place, so this was later changed to Peacehaven. In the original plan, dated 1916, for Anzac-on-Sea, many of the streets were named after First World War battles: Louvain, Marne, Mons, Loos, Festubert, Salonica and Ypres Avenues. These were later changed to: Gladys, Sunview, Vernon, Southdown, Seaview and Friars Avenues. It was obviously not possible to sell plots of land on avenues bearing names which reminded people of the tragedies of these First World War battles."

Lucy Noakes
Blighty Brighton

(106) Caravan, Rushey Hill Caravan Park, 2019.

(107) Gas bottle, Rushey Hill Caravan Park, 2019.

OUTSKIRTS - CONTRIBUTORS

Leila Abrahams, We're Not All Rothschilds! The Extraordinary Lives Of Some Ordinary Jews (1994). Exploring the lives of ordinary working people linked by their Jewish faith.

Mary Adams, Those Lost Years, (1995). From a wartime childhood in convent schools to an adult life at St Marye's, and a burgeoning independence.

Aileen, Daring Hearts, (1992). QueenSpark Books in collaboration with Brighton Ourstory. The definitive guide to queer life in Brighton in the 1950s and 1960s in a collection of life stories.

Hilda Barber, Blighty Brighton, (1991). Photographs and memories of Brighton in the First World War.

Marjory Batchelor, A Life Behind Bars, (1999). A working life spent as a barmaid and pub landlady.

Brighton & Hove's Bangladeshi community, Bangla Brighton, (2006). A series of moving accounts of life on the South coast by Brighton and Hove's Bangladeshi community.

Don Carter, Just One Of A Large Family, (1992). Memories of growing up in the Hartington Road area of Brighton, beginning in the 1920s.

Barbara Chapman, Boxing Day Baby, (1994). A personal impression of growing up and working in Brighton in the 1930s and 1940s.

Joyce Collins, Blighty Brighton, (1991). Photographs and memories of Brighton in the First World War.

Michael Corum, Blighty Brighton, (1991). Photographs and memories of Brighton in the First World War.

Ruby Dunn, Moulsecoomb Days. 1922-1947, (1990). A first-person account of a close-knit community.

Dorothy Fuller, Write From The Beginning, (2002). An anthology containing work from the Vallance Memories Group and the Brunswick Older People's Project.

Nat Gilroy, We're Not All Rothschilds! The Extraordinary Lives Of Some Ordinary Jews, (1994). Based around interviews by Leila Abrahams in Brighton & Hove exploring the lives of ordinary working people linked by their Jewish faith.

Louis and Bernie Goldberg, We're Not All Rothschilds! The Extraordinary Lives Of Some Ordinary Jews, (1994). An exploration of the lives of ordinary working people linked by their Jewish faith.

George Grout, The Smiling Bakers, (1992). A recollection of life and work at the bakery on Coombe Road, between 1900 and the Second World War.

Bert Healey, Hard Times And Easy Terms, (1980). Tales of his wayward boyhood in Brighton during the First World War, and a description of his working life.

Dave Huggins, Back Row Brighton, (2009). Recollections of cinema-going in Brighton and Hove between the 1930s and the 1960s.

Mrs Jackson, Back Street Brighton, (1989). Photographs taken by the Environmental Health Department in the late 1940s and early 1950s of houses in Brighton that were scheduled for demolition in the

1950s and the 1960s. The photographs are accompanied by reminiscences of families who lived in the houses.

Keith Jago, Remember the First Time? A collection of Childhood memories, (2002). Eight writers share memories of their childhood.

Alan Jeal, Back Street Brighton, (1989). Photographs taken by the Environmental Health Department in the late 1940s and early 1950s of houses in Brighton that were scheduled for demolition in the 1950s and 1960s. The photographs are accompanied by reminiscences of families who lived in the houses.

John Knight, A Ha'p'orth Of Sweets, (1997). Growing up in the Albion Hill area of Brighton in the 1930s and 1940s.

Georgiana Lally, Brighton Behind the Front, (1990). Portraying life during the Second World War using a collection of personal recollections, photographs, letters, a logbook and diaries.

John Langley, Always A Layman, (1976). Describing his childhood in poverty before the First World War, work as a railway carriage painter, and activism in the Labour movement.

Len Liechti, Back Row Brighton, (2009). Recollections of cinema-going in Brighton and Hove between the 1930s and the 1960s.

Sid Manville, Everything Seems Smaller: A Brighton Boyhood Between the Wars, (1989). Growing up around Bear Road.

Sid Manville, Our Small Corner, (1994). Growing up around Bear Road, a sequel to Everything Seems Smaller.

Margaret, Daring Hearts, (1992). QueenSpark Books in collaboration with Brighton Ourstory. The definitive guide to queer life in Brighton in the 1950s and 1960s in a collection of life stories.

Ernie Mason, A Working Man - A Century Of Hove Memories, (1998). From his earliest childhood memories in 1910, to a varied working life in Hove.

Les McLenahan, letter to Whitehawk Then And Now, Sparchives, Queenspark Newspaper No. 29 Winter 1981.

Daisy Noakes, The Town Beehive, (1975). Growing up around Ditchling Road, and an early working life in service in the 1920s.

Lucy Noakes, Blighty Brighton, (1991). Photographs and memories of Brighton in the First World War.

Maurice Packman, The Church Round The Corner, (2000). Memories of a boyhood as a choirboy in the 1930s, and the social and religious history of St Anne's Church.

Albert Paul, Poverty: Hardship But Happiness, Those Were The Days 1903-1917, (1974). Growing up in the Hanover area of Brighton.

Albert Paul, Hard Work And No Consideration, 51 Years As A Carpenter-Joiner 1917-1968, (1981). Describing his hard work and commitment through the recession of the 1920s to the post war period, and on to the 1960s, a sequel to Poverty: Hardship but Happiness.

Ron Piper, Take Him Away, (1995). From a seven year old looking for shrapnel on bomb sites in London during the second World War to a career criminal in the dock at The Old Bailey.

Father of three, picture framer, member of East Brighton Residents Association, QueenSpark Rates Book Group, Brighton On The Rocks, Monetarism And The Local State, (1983). An analysis of public spending decisions and outcomes for Brighton.

QueenSpark Rates Book Group, Brighton On The Rocks, Monetarism And The Local State, (1983). An analysis of public spending decisions and outcomes for Brighton.

Janis Ravenett, Snapshots, Childhood Memories Of Southampton Street 1942-1955, (1996). Growing up from a child's point of view.

Sandie, Daring Hearts, (1992). QueenSpark Books in collaboration with Brighton Ourstory. The definitive guide to queer life in Brighton in the 1950s and 1960s in a collection of life stories.

Lottie Scarborough, Blighty Brighton, (1991). Photographs and memories of Brighton in the First World War.

Corinne Silver, We're Not All Rothschilds! The Extraordinary Lives Of Some Ordinary Jews, (1994). An exploration of the lives of ordinary working people.

Andie Steer, Brighton Boy, A Fifties Childhood, (1994). A child's-eye view of post-war Brighton.

Mark Stephenson, introduction to Ernie Mason, A Working Man - A Century Of Hove Memories, (1998). From his earliest childhood memory in 1910, to a varied working life in Hove.

Vera, Daring Hearts, (1992). QueenSpark Books in collaboration with Brighton Ourstory. The definitive guide to queer life in Brighton in the 1950s and 1960s in a collection of life stories.

Margaret Ward, One Camp Chair In The Living Room, (1988). From a childhood in Rottingdean in the aftermath of the first World War, through to marriage and retirement.

Margaret Ward, Memories Of Rottingdean, 1920-1945, (1993). A first person snapshot of rural Sussex life.

Kathleen Wilson, International Service, (2002). Adolescence, life and work in Brighton in the 1940s and 1950s.

Michael and Leslie Wilson, A Far Cry From A White Apron, The Story Of A Brighton Bevin Boy, (2000). From shop assistant to working in a Welsh coal mine during the Second World War.

Sheila Winter, Moulsecoomb Memories: Moulsecoomb In The 1930s and '40s, (1998). A memoir recalling the growth of the community of Moulsecoomb.

Tim Wren, Flying Sparks, (1998). An autobiography of an electrician, beginning his apprenticeship during the First World War.

PHOTO REFERENCES

(Front cover) View east from Black Rock to the Marina, 2019 by Vicky Waters.

(Back cover) Black Rock swimming pool, 1961. Royal Pavilion & Museums.

(Shoreham) Lancing Carriage Works, 1963 by Ian Nolan.

(Portslade) Postcard showing Railway Inn on Station Road, c.1907. Royal Pavilion & Museums.

(Devil's Dyke and The Downs) Postcard showing 'The Kops', c.1930. Royal Pavilion & Museums.

(Hove) Hove Town Hall, 2019 by Vicky Waters.

(Withdean and Patcham) Unveiling of Chattri memorial, 1 February 1921. Royal Pavilion & Museums.

(Preston Park) At the entrance to Preston Park, 2019 by Vicky Waters.

(Hollingbury) Hollingbury Hillfort, 2019 by Vicky Waters.

(Coldean) Parkside Estate, Coldean, 1940s. Royal Pavilion & Museums.

(Moulsecoomb) A civic function on the Moulsecoomb housing estate at Hodshrove Road, Brighton, c.1930s. Royal Pavilion & Museums.

(Hollingdean) The Ohel in Florence Place Cemetery, 2019 by Vicky Waters.

(Elm Grove and Bear Road) Woodvale Cemetery, 2016 by Michèle Allardyce.

(Bevendean & Racehill) Lower Bevendean Estate, c.1940s. Royal Pavilion & Museums.

(Whitehawk) Brighton Transport: Double Decker Bus No 3 Whitehawk. Royal Pavilion & Museums.

(Black Rock) Subway between Black Rock and the Marina, 2019 by Vicky Waters.

(Woodingdean) Woodingdean prefab estate, 1953. Royal Pavilion & Museums.

(Rottingdean) Aerial view of Rottingdean, 1930s. Royal Pavilion & Museums.

(Saltdean) Rock groyne, Saltdean, 2019 by Vicky Waters.

(Peacehaven) Peacehaven Heights, Peacehaven, 2019 by Vicky Waters.

(1) By Ian Nolan
(2) By Vicky Waters
(3) By Vicky Waters
(4) By Vicky Waters
(5) By Vicky Waters
(6) Royal Pavilion & Museums
(7) By Vicky Waters
(8) By Vicky Waters
(9) By Vicky Waters
(10) By Vicky Waters
(11) By Simon Carey
(12) By Vicky Waters
(13) Royal Pavilion & Museums
(14) By Vicky Waters
(15) Royal Pavilion & Museums
(16) Royal Pavilion & Museums
(17) By Vicky Waters
(18) Royal Pavilion & Museums
(19) By Vicky Waters
(20) By Michèle Allardyce
(21) By Vicky Waters
(22) By Vicky Waters
(23) By Vicky Waters
(24) The James Gray Collection
(25) By Vicky Waters
(26) By The Voice of Hassocks
(27) By Vicky Waters
(28) By Vicky Waters
(29) By Vicky Waters
(30) By Vicky Waters

(31) By Vicky Waters
(32) By Vicky Waters
(33) By Vicky Waters
(34) Royal Pavilion & Museums
(35) Royal Pavilion & Museums
(36) By Vicky Waters
(37) By Vicky Waters
(38) By Vicky Waters
(39) Royal Pavilion & Museums
(40) Royal Pavilion & Museums
(41) By Vicky Waters
(42) By Vicky Waters
(43) Royal Pavilion & Museums
(44) By Dusashenka
(45) Royal Pavilion & Museums
(46) By Barry Pitman
(47) By Barry Pitman
(48) Royal Pavilion & Museums
(49) Royal Pavilion & Museums
(50) Royal Pavilion & Museums
(51) By Vicky Waters
(52) Royal Pavilion & Museums
(53) By Vicky Waters
(54) By Michèle Allardyce
(55) By Vicky Waters
(56) By Vicky Waters
(57) By Vicky Waters
(58) Royal Pavilion & Museums
(59) By Vicky Waters
(60) Royal Pavilion & Museums
(61) Royal Pavilion & Museums
(62) By Vicky Waters
(63) By Vicky Waters
(64) By Vicky Waters
(65) By Vicky Waters
(66) By Michèle Allardyce
(67) Royal Pavilion & Museums
(68) James Gray Collection
(69) James Gray Collection
(70) By Vicky Waters
(71) Royal Pavilion & Museums
(72) Royal Pavilion & Museums
(73) By Vicky Waters
(74) By Vicky Waters
(75) James Gray Collection
(76) Royal Pavilion & Museums
(77) By Vicky Waters
(78) Royal Pavilion & Museums
(79) By Michèle Allardyce
(80) By Michèle Allardyce
(81) By Michèle Allardyce
(82) By Michèle Allardyce
(83) Royal Pavilion & Museums
(84) By Vicky Waters
(85) Royal Pavilion & Museums
(86) By Vicky Waters
(87) By Michèle Allardyce
(88) By Michèle Allardyce
(89) By Vicky Waters
(90) Royal Pavilion & Museums
(91) By Vicky Waters
(92) By Vicky Waters
(93) By Vicky Waters
(94) Royal Pavilion & Museums
(95) By Vicky Waters
(96) By Michèle Allardyce
(97) Royal Pavilion & Museums
(98) Royal Pavilion & Museums
(99) By Vicky Waters
(100) By Vicky Waters
(101) By Vicky Waters
(102) By Vicky Waters
(103) By Vicky Waters
(104) Lido Community Interest Company
(105) By Vicky Waters
(106) By Vicky Waters
(107) By Vicky Waters
(108) By Michèle Allardyce

MAP PHOTOS (Clockwise from top left)

Devil's Dyke railway, c.1940s.
Royal Pavilion & Museums.

Devil's Dyke trolley bus.
Royal Pavilion & Museums.

Dedication of the Indian
Chattri by HRH the Prince of
Wales on the Downs, Feb 1921.
Royal Pavilion & Museums.

Double Decker Trolley Bus No 26
Hollinbury, at the Old Steine,
Brighton, c.1939. Royal Pavilion
& Museums.

Tram shelter, Queen's Park Road,
2019 by Vicky Waters.

Woodvale Cemetery, 2016
by Michèle Allardyce.

Lower Bevendean Estate, c.1940s.
Royal Pavilion & Museums.

Tram shelter, Ditchling Road,
2019 by Vicky Waters.

Rottingdean, The Beach & Slipway.
Royal Pavilion & Museums.

Brighton Racecourse, c.1956.
Royal Pavilion & Museums.

Black Rock swimming pool, 1961.
Royal Pavilion & Museums.

Brighton Transport: Double Decker
Bus No 3 Whitehawk. Royal Pavilion
& Museums.

Postcard showing Railway Inn on
Station Road, c.1907. Royal Pavilion
& Museums.

Site of Holland Road Halt, 2006
by Simon Carey.

(Large photo) Railway sleepers
beside the path that follows the
old rail route to Devil's Dyke,
2019 by Vicky Waters.

(108) Bellflower (Campanula),
picked and pressed, May 2019.

ACKNOWLEDGEMENTS

Published by QueenSpark Books, a charity which, since 1972, has helped the people of Brighton & Hove to tell their stories.

QueenSpark Books gratefully acknowledges the financial assistance of The National Lottery Heritage Fund, which made possible the Archives Alive project, and Brighton & Hove City Council and the University of Brighton for their ongoing support. With gratitude to all the volunteers and participants in Archives Alive.

Copyright © 2019 QueenSpark Books and the authors and contributors
Brighton's Outskirts - people, place, community

All rights reserved. No part of this publication may be reproduced without written permission, except in the case of brief extracts embodied in articles, reviews or lectures.

First published in Great Britain in 2019 by QueenSpark Books, Brighton, UK.

A catalogue record for this book is available from the British Library
ISBN 978-1-9996699-3-5

Designer Emily Macaulay
www.stanleyjamespress.com

Managing Editor John Riches

Developmental Editors Kevin Bacon (Photographs), Evlynn Sharp (Text)

Editors Michèle Allardyce and Vicky Waters

Photo Editors Ali Ghanimi, Barry Pitman, Helen Smedley

Photography Michèle Allardyce and Vicky Waters © 2019

Map artwork Michèle Allardyce

Map OpenStreetMap © OpenStreetMap contributors https://www.openstreetmap.org/copyright
The OpenStreetMap data is available under the Open Database Licence, and in relation to map tiles, the cartography is licensed as CC BY-SA.

Image archives James Gray Collection, QueenSpark Books, Regency Society, Royal Pavilion and Museums, Brighton & Hove

Printed by One Digital, Woodingdean
www.one-digital.com

QueenSpark Books

admin@queensparkbooks.org.uk
Web www.queensparkbooks.org.uk
Registered Charity Number 1172938
Company Number 02404473

Copyright disclaimer: Writing and images by kind permission of authors, photographers, and other sources, where possible. QueenSpark Books has made efforts to ensure that the reproduction of content in this publication is done with the full consent of copyright holders. If you feel that your copyright has not been fully respected, please contact us by email:
admin@queensparkbooks.org.uk